Salesians – Contemplatives in Action

Michael J Cunningham SDB

ISBN 978-1-909080-15-7

– for my Salesian brothers and sisters

Contents

Foreward

The present book by Michael Cunningham is a welcome addition to the Salesian literature which is steadily growing in these last few years. In view of 2015, the second centenary of the birth of Don Bosco, Michael's reflections will enrich all those among us who, through these chapters, can deepen the spirituality of Don Bosco in today's post-modern context.

Michael is no newcomer in the field of spiritual reflection. This book is a gift that benefits from his years of ministry, retreats and spiritual direction, and also his writing. So it is with great joy that I offer the following reflections.

There are two things which stay with me after reading the different chapters. The first one is the way Michael presents the mystical experience as central to our faith life. The recovery of the mystical experience is going to determine our future and it will shape, in a profound way, our ministry. The references to the various stages of the history of the Church, necessarily brief but effective, strengthen the conviction that, unless we recover the centre, we will lose our identity and the power to bring light and hope to the young.

At the centre, lies the experience of God's love, the personal encounter with a God who reaches us, embraces us, in the person of Jesus. Don Bosco is an icon and a shining example of someone who has experienced God's divine love within his own story. Making this experience central to his existence, Don Bosco made sure that his experience became that of many. Mary Mazzarello, in her own unique way, takes up this story and develops it, for the benefit of many. Each one of us, in her and his own way, is also invited to make sure to enter this second phase of mystery: where the human story opens itself up to God's mystic love.

The second aspect, which I appreciated when reading this book, is the way Michael combines the heritage of the Salesian tradition, constitutions, and letters by the various successors of Don Bosco and Mary Mazzarello. He unfolds this treasure in a way that the central theme becomes even more *Salesian* with every page. I believe that this exercise is also a lesson for us all: that is, to discover the value of our Salesian tradition in the various reflections offered to the Salesian Congregation, especially those contained in the letters of our last three Rector Majors. The insights and reflections offered in these pages carry a certain vitality which Michael has beautifully presented in a unified manner. May this effort encourage each one of us not only to be happy with our heritage, but to promote it when so many young people are looking for wisdom and friendship through our educative ministry.

I would like to thank Michael for this work. May God bless his ministry and the ministry of all those who, like him, as good disciples of the kingdom have the gift of bringing out treasures of wisdom.

Fr Fabio Attard SDB

Councillor for Youth Ministry

GENERAL COUNCIL OF THE SALESIANS OF DON BOSCO

6th May 2012

Introduction

We are with Don Bosco and the times,
not with the times of Don Bosco.[1]

On December 19th 2009, the Rector Major, Fr Pascual Chávez, gave what he called *a keynote address* in Valdocco to commemorate the 150th anniversary of the founding of the Salesian Congregation. He spoke to representative groups of the Salesian family gathered in Turin for the celebrations. His aim was to strengthen the spiritual and apostolic identity of those who try to live the Salesian charism. I want to begin this book by quoting, at length, what I consider to be the most challenging aspect of his words:

> With a view to overcoming spiritual mediocrity, which deprives us of the ability to have an attitude and outlook of faith, it is absolutely necessary to know, understand and live Don Bosco's spirituality. Many times I have repeated that we know his life story which has been studied a great deal by our historians, and also his pedagogical method studied in depth by his educationalists; whereas we know much less about his spiritual experience and his spirituality.
>
> Knowledge about the events of Don Bosco's life, of his activities and of his educational method is not enough. At the basis of everything, as the source of the fruitfulness of his work and relevance, there is something which often escapes us – his profound spiritual experience, what we can call his familiarity with God. We should not be surprised that Don Bosco's spirituality has been described as *continuous union with God*, tireless activity sanctified by prayer and union with God.
>
> A really profound spiritual life is not possible without daily familiarity with the word of God and the Eucharist, which constitute the essential centre of the life of an apostle and a community of apostles.
>
> Without this familiarity we can easily slip into activism which only produces psychological stress, physical tiredness and

1 Fr Egidio Viganò

exhaustion (*burnout*), insensitivity to the needs of others, and spiritual superficiality. Activism can rightly be called the new heresy, making us think that everything depends on us, our activity, that we can do without God, forgetting what Jesus said: *Without me you can do nothing.*[2]

The time has come to give back to the Spirit the primary role that is his and to recover the primacy of grace. Only in this way is an experience of God possible, without which there is no Salesian mission since this consists not in doing things but in being *signs of God's love.* We therefore have to take care of our intimacy with the Lord Jesus which makes us loving disciples and enthusiastic apostles.

It is obvious therefore that we need to pray and transform our activity in prayer, to the point where we become *contemplatives in action.*[3]

In this book I wish to share some reflections on how we Salesians might respond to these words of the Rector Major and in particular to the call for us to become *contemplatives in action*, and to live Don Bosco's own spirituality of continuous union with God. My reflections are, necessarily, personal and limited, but I hope they stimulate some reflection on the need to restore the balance in our lives between action and prayer. It is with this *balance* in mind that I chose the graphic on the front cover - the young energetic John Bosco discovering new ways of winning over young people, prepared to take every risk for them, but who discovered the balance in his life. I hope this evocative graphic will continue to remind us of the balance needed in our lives, as we work with young people.

As Salesians, we like to think of ourselves as men and women of action. In my lifetime, as a Salesian, I have now heard three successors of Don Bosco warn against the danger of excessive activism. Fr Viganò reminded us often about the dangers of superficiality creeping into our busy lives and he spoke about the need to balance our activity with our prayer life in what he called *the grace of unity*. I recall Fr Vecchi quoting the words of the twentieth-century theologian Karl Rahner that

---

2 Jn 15.8

3 Fr Pascual Chávez *Acts of the General Council* (May-August 2010) p84-85

the Christian of the future will either be a mystic, or he will cease to exist. And now Fr Chávez is challenging us to become contemplatives in action. Similar advice has been given to the Salesian Sisters by Mother Antonia Colombo and the present Mother General, Yvonne Reungoat.

We are living in times in which a dangerous gap has been opening up between *religion* and *spirituality*. Many thinking people today describe themselves as *spiritual* but not *religious*. There seems to be a deep hunger in people's lives – in their souls, in fact – that institutional religion is not meeting. I think that this hunger, however vaguely felt, seeks a connection with Ultimate Reality, what we call God, and the revival of the contemplative tradition is one way of meeting that hunger. When we give ourselves to that search, we discover that our yearning for God is God's yearning for us. It is the same yearning because this is why we have been created.

In this book I have tried to outline an adult Salesian spirituality, one that faces some of the challenges of our time. I see the dream of Don Bosco as an evolving dream that needs to be lived in new ways in these liminal times, in which we find ourselves. I have reflected on how we can understand the Preventive System as a spirituality that leads us through the agenda for the first-half of life, which if negotiated properly, leads us into the transition point of life's crises of suffering, failure, inconsistencies, injustice and woundedness, to emerge hopefully into the second-half of life's agenda characterised by compassion, mercy, and forgiveness, what Don Bosco called loving-kindness – Bontà.

This pattern can be traced in the biblical literature of Law, Prophets and Wisdom. It marks the movement from religion as morality, to spirituality as mysticism. It is a movement into *both/and* spirituality rather than *either/or* spirituality, and each stage must be included in the journey to spiritual maturity. In order to reach the second-half of life we have to be transformed by great love, great suffering and prayer. It is prayer, particularly contemplative prayer, that I have reflected on as we are being called to become active contemplatives.

I have included numerous quotations usually as chapter headings from sources such as Rectors Major, Mothers General, Chapter documents from both congregations, and both SDB and FMA Constitutions, encouraging us in this challenge, to achieve a better balance in our busy lives. We know that both Don Bosco and Mary Mazzarello lived very active lives but at the same time they experienced a deep union with God. As far as I am aware they did not teach contemplative prayer, and I suggest that this is largely because they lived at a time when the whole contemplative tradition was almost lost to the Western Church. Today we are seeing a revival of contemplation, not just as a way of praying but as a new way of seeing. The great gift of our age is that what was once known to a few mystics is now being experienced by many people including the laity. The Sacred Masculine agenda of the first-half of life – law, rules, order, hierarchy, reason, autonomy – is being united with the second-half of life agenda – compassion, mercy, forgiveness, communion – with what is being called the Sacred Feminine, and Mary, the Mother of Jesus, is at the heart of this awareness.

The recovery of the contemplative tradition is moving us beyond the dualistic agenda of the ego, which is constantly making judgements about who is right and who is wrong, who is up and who is down, us and them, Catholic and non-Catholic, to the non-dual teaching of Jesus that he called the kingdom of God: that we are one with God, one with all people, and one with creation rather than separate, isolated individuals.

One of the most encouraging signs of our times is the amazing discoveries of our scientists about the nature of the universe and the many mysteries that lie out there in space and time, emphasising our need to care for the earth. We are being challenged to move beyond our rather limited concentration on ourselves, to unite our personal stories with the larger story of our planet and the universe, in which we find ourselves, as an unfolding mystery.

The scientists are confirming that it is a profoundly relational story and spiritual teachers are calling it a mystery of participation. If we can get to the second-half of life our task is to pass on what little wisdom we have learned about our amazing relational Trinitarian God who seeks an intimate friendship with each one of us, despite our woundedness. Our task is to live the evolving dream of Don Bosco which is included in God's dream for all humanity, as it unfolds in our souls, in our communities, and in creation. I suggest that the integration of the active and contemplative life is the great challenge facing religious life in these times.

I offer these reflections on adult Salesian spirituality after forty eight years of Salesian religious life with a lot of humility, in the hope that they may stimulate those far better qualified than me to do likewise as we approach the bicentenary of our founder's birth.

Michael Cunningham SDB

Holy Week 2012

Chapter 1 – The First-Half of Life

> What is the normal goal to the young person becomes a neurotic hindrance by old age. We cannot live the afternoon of life according to the programme of life's morning. For what was great in the morning will be of little importance by the evening. And what, in the morning, was true will by the evening have actually become a lie.[4]

> Very truly I tell you, when you were younger you dressed yourself and went where you wanted; but when you are old you will stretch out your hands, and someone else will dress you and lead you where you do not want to go.[5]

There is a necessary tension written into Salesian spirituality. I think it is reflected in the lives of all people; but for Salesians, who work with and for the young, it is particularly acute. We are supposed to be experts in youth spirituality and youth ministry, but there can be a danger for adults working with the young that our own spirituality doesn't grow and mature as we move through life. Carl Jung's words highlight the problem, and I have added the words of Jesus in case you think this is just a bit of psychology, masquerading as spirituality. The suggestion is that there are two different journeys to be discovered and undertaken in life. Once we discover this, some of our problems with religion and spirituality start to disappear. What I want to reflect on, in this opening chapter, is a new way of looking at Don Bosco's Preventive System, to guide us through the necessary challenges.

Moving beyond the agenda for the first-half of life is not an easy task and its difficulty may explain why many Christians do not make the journey to the maturity of the second-half of life. Jesus warns us how challenging this can be when he taught that we have to lose our life if we are to really find it. The disciples found this very difficult to accept and Peter led the opposition – *No, Lord, this must never happen to you –*

---

4 Carl Jung *The Structure and Dynamics of the Psyche*

5 Jn 21.18

only to be addressed as *Satan* by Jesus. We shouldn't be too hard on Peter. We all find it difficult.

There is plenty of evidence in scripture to support the idea that there is some clear staging in the spiritual journey. The letter to the Hebrews suggests that many of them have not grown spiritually; they are still in the first-half of life:

> By this time, you ought to be teachers yourselves, yet here I find you need someone to sit down with you and go over the basics on God again starting from square one – baby's milk, when you should have been on solid food long ago! Milk is for beginners, inexperienced in God's ways; solid food is for the mature who have some practice in telling what's right from what's really wrong.[6]

There is a vivid contrast of a religion of baby's milk with one that provides solid food. Only then can we really discern what is really right from what is really wrong. John suggests a different contrast between a religion based on fear of God with one of love:

> There is no fear in love, but perfect love casts out fear; for fear has to do with punishment, and whoever fears has not reached perfection in love.[7]

Both Paul and John, therefore, see clear staging in the spiritual life, from milk to solid food or from fear to love. Jesus' words at the head of the chapter make the same point, contrasting youthful spirituality with adult spirituality. The American scripture scholar, Walter Brueggemann, sees this staging reflected in the books of the bible, from Law to Wisdom via the Prophets, and I think that Don Bosco's own pattern of *Reason, Religion and Loving-kindness*, his Preventive System, shows the same kind of development.

As we look in more detail at this, it is worth noting that there are many secular texts that reinforce the same message. These are the great legends and mythologies of literature such as Homer's Odyssey, and many of the Quest stories recorded by

---

6 Heb 5:12-14 scripture taken from *The Message* (2003) used with permission of Navpress
7 1 Jn 4:18

Joseph Campbell,[8] recalling the hero's journey away from his homeland, his adventures, failures and struggles before his return home in triumph with a new wisdom to share with his community. It's interesting to see that this ancient wisdom of two journeys was discerned long before Christianity appeared on the scene. Inspired storytellers intuited what religion should formally teach. In recent times the Franciscan, Richard Rohr, has drawn on much of this sacred and secular material in his insightful book on first and second-half-of-life spirituality, and I am indebted to him for many of the ideas that shape this chapter.[9]

The world today is undergoing a most profound period of change. In the past we saw religion as a kind of bulwark against change, and that is probably why religion was often a conservative force in times of upheaval. Don Bosco himself was caught up in times of political upheaval in nineteenth-century Italy and some of his views were conservative. At the same time, he had very radical ideas about a new religious family that would serve the needs of poor and abandoned young people. Like all spiritually-mature people, I suggest he was able to live the second-half-of-life agenda because he had lived the first-half well and lived the necessary creative tension.

I want to set out this pattern of spiritual growth as a key task for life. The agenda for the second-half of life is the true task within the task. Without it, I don't think we can be true educators. It builds on the task for the first-half of life but if we stay locked at that level of development we get stuck with the container rather than its contents. We end up with a rather legalistic view of religion, concerned with correct formulas, correct words and correct performance. Nowhere in the Gospels does Jesus say *Thou shalt be correct.* The whole purpose of a mature spirituality is to distinguish between the container and the contents. This is making the step from religion as *morality*, to religion as *mysticism;* when it becomes authentic spirituality. Before looking at this more closely we need to remind ourselves that some young people get into the

---

8 Joseph Campbell *The Hero with a Thousand Faces* (NJ Princeton University Press 1949)

9 Richard Rohr *Falling Upward* (Jossey-Bass San Francisco 2011)

second-half-of-life agenda very early in life, while, sadly, some older people never reach it. These are not rigid divisions.

The Law (*Reason*)

When we look at the first few books of the bible we see a clear emphasis on the Law, the Torah. There are many other themes in these books but the importance of the Law seems to take prominence. Books like Genesis, Exodus, Leviticus, Numbers and Deuteronomy don't always make easy reading. I've often suggested to people who take sleeping pills to throw them away and try reading the book of Leviticus. These books, however, record the struggle of human beings to connect with and gain some insight into the mystery of God. They wisely begin by trying to lay a solid foundation in the search for God. They stress the need for tradition, security, boundaries, clarity, control of impulses, order and the building up of a strong ego identity. It is the construction of the necessary container.

Parents will be well aware of this task, and those of us who have worked in school ministry will be equally aware of the need young people have for order and discipline. The emphasis is on religion as morality. The young need clear guidance as to what is right and what is wrong and Don Bosco with his stress on reason wanted adults to use the key virtues of the second-half of life (loving-kindness, compassion, mercy and love) to help the young person negotiate this first stage well. Hence Don Bosco's stress on explaining why rules and regulations exist rather than seek slavish enforcement.

One of the important aspects of the first-half of life's journey is to make the young feel valued and affirmed. This is necessary for all people but especially those who have been abandoned and rejected. Salesians often quote Don Bosco's advice that the young should not only be loved but genuinely feel they are loved and accepted. The early books of the bible illustrate this need, by stressing that this small tribe of Hebrews has been specially chosen by God. At the same time this positive affirmation can have negative effects, because if Israel has become the chosen people they quickly conclude that other people and other tribes have not been chosen by God. This kind of exclusivism all too easily promotes an ethnocentric or tribal understanding of God. By assuming that we Catholics are God's chosen ones in succession to the Jews, we have often fallen into a similar restrictive view. We are the saved, others such as Protestants, or Muslims are not. Remember the line, *Outside the Church, no salvation.* Don Bosco's time was characterised by Counter-Reformation suspicion and even open rivalry between different faiths. I think Don Bosco would be a leading advocate of ecumenism today. Certainly we Salesians can promote it in his name.

It is, of course, normal and natural to bring up the young to value and love their faith tradition. Today that pride in faith identity needs to be less exclusive and to recognise that God loves all people and to recognise the famous line of Peter in the Acts, *Today I learned that God has no favourites.* This is a second-half-of-life statement, but the Church hasn't always taught this and it was only as recently as Vatican II that we formally recognised the good in other non-Christian religions. Pope John Paul's meeting with the leaders of all the world religions at Assisi in 1986 wasn't universally popular at the time. So, by all means, let us inculcate a real pride in our faith tradition and our Salesian tradition, among our young people, but let it not be in a triumphalist sense of superiority. I have often related how my brother and I when we were growing up were laughing at the local Salvation Army Band. My Dad gave us a very forceful telling-off; reminding us of all the good work the Salvation Army did for the poor. Years later, when I entered a Salvation Army pulpit to give a Lenten talk on asylum seekers, I couldn't help but remember those words.

The Covenant

The spiritual journey negotiated successfully leads to a deep and lasting discovery of God's unconditional love. We realise, later in life, that God's gift has already been given. At every moment of our existence we are held in God's unconditional love. The problem is that we are not conscious of it. Hopefully good parenting and good teaching provides us glimpses of this kind of love, but we live in an imperfect world and not even the best of parents and teachers can convince us at all times. We need the experience of conditional love to get us through the first-half of life, to help us in what spiritual teachers call *The dance of survival.* Later there will be a more rewarding dance to enjoy.

This was also true for the people of Israel. As Yahweh led the people out of Egypt, he wanted to reinforce their still-fragile faith and so at Mount Sinai and in the wilderness the people accepted God's covenant. It was a kind of deal to remind them that they would have to keep God's commandments in return for his protection. It urged them to live morally, and the great sign of this was the Ten Commandments, although there were many other commandments in those first books of the bible – scholars have counted over six hundred. These are necessary laws for social order. We expect people to tell the truth, not to steal, to show respect to parents and elders and so on. It's a good start but it is not the whole journey.

The first-half of life journey tends to highlight morality, rules, law and order. Keep all the rules and God will reward you and life will go well. In my early Salesian formation we were told, *Keep the Rule and the Rule will keep you.* Unfortunately it tends to suggest that God's love has to be earned by our good behaviour. I think it is true to say that most Christians are still living the first-half of life agenda, what Paul rather dismissively called *baby's milk*.

This kind of faith tends to be rather individualistic and self-centred. It led us to talk a lot, about *saving our souls.* The most important thing was to get to heaven. There was little emphasis on trying to live a life of union with God on earth, little teaching on the mystical path to union. Religion became a kind of insurance policy rather than an invitation to a spiritual adventure. And for us Salesians that pushed us further into the agenda of constant activity, because we had to work hard for our salvation, to get God to like us, to win his approval. We have always been encouraged to pray, but our prayer was largely made up of *saying prayers* and we were rarely, if at all, invited to a more contemplative way of praying. The problem here is that the ego can then take control and however hard we work and pray we still remain in the ego-led first-half of life. Perhaps it was concerns like this behind the Rector Major's comment in a letter to Salesians in 2003:

> Not infrequently, in visiting the Congregation, I have come across confreres brimful of apostolic energy and courage who

> are immersed in amazing works for the benefit of youngsters, but who do not seem motivated and animated by a similar zeal for God. If, on the one hand, one cannot but admire their dedication; on the other one cannot help wondering what is the real motive force behind such great activity.[10]

Such an imbalance leaves us trapped in a religion that emphasises the performance principle and leaves us with little experience of the Great Mystery, the Great Compassion, the Great Love which is the goal of all mature religion and spirituality. Nevertheless we cannot and should not avoid the first-half of life agenda. You have to have an ego in order to grow beyond the ego, to be ready for the spacious mystery that Jesus calls the kingdom of God, which we are invited to experience in this life not just in eternity.

Healthy growth is always a matter of *transcend* and *include;* it is *both/and* not *either/or.* This leads us into the higher consciousness of the second-half-of-life agenda, when we get to taste the wine. Our Salesian activity becomes sacred activity, a primary meeting place for us with the divine. Our doing is integrated with our being as we begin to form the *false ego-self* to the *true-self,* which is the soul. This is what we understand today as *saving our souls.* It is the transition from ego-centric living to soul-centric living. But for that to happen something has to die. When the first-half of life is done well we can approach this death with courage, faith and love rather than fear. If it is done badly it leaves us trapped with a distant God who is only interested in reward and punishments, a religion of fear. No wonder many people today walk away from that agenda, dissatisfied.

10 Fr Pascual Chávez *Acts of the General Council* (July-September 2003) p6

Chapter 2 – The Path of Transition

It is a hard road and a narrow gate that leads to life.[11]

The second element of Don Bosco's Preventive System is the word *religion*. We believers tend to think that religion is always a source of good and, as evangelisers, we want to convert the whole world to religious belief. In our culture today we need to be more critical. We look back at the Enlightenment and see it as a bleak period when the enthronement of reason challenged the influence of religion and greatly reduced its influence in the Western World. Yet we have to acknowledge that it was a reaction to the violence of the Reformation when Christians tortured and killed each other in the name of Jesus. *Remember the cruelties*, was the cry of Voltaire. We cannot deny that religion has been – and still is – in many parts of the world a contributing factor in wars, divisions and conflicts. At the same time many thoughtful people are recognising that pure secularism and atheism don't really feed the soul or help us to confront the deeper mysteries of love, truth, beauty, suffering, loss and death.

Today many searchers for meaning turn not to religion; but to spirituality. An unhealthy gap is emerging as our pews continue to empty. This is a challenge for us believers, and for those of us who work in the education of the young. We have to give them credible reasons for belief and practice. I think that the recognition that there are stages in the spiritual journey can be a useful way to guide us through the difficult path of growth to maturity. It requires that we adults have faced the challenge of growth and can see the difference between healthy and unhealthy religion.

There has been a lot of scholarly work in recent years on the idea of development, of different levels of consciousness and awareness. There is the work of James Fowler, Lawrence Kohlberg, Carol Gilligan, Ken Wilber, Clare Graves, Don Beck and Bill Plotkin. As we saw in chapter one this kind of development was intuited by the writers of the scriptures, and Jesus himself long before Freud and Jung appeared on the

11 Mt 7:14

scene, was talking about the need for shadow awareness – *if you want to take the splinter out of your brother's eye take the plank out of your own!* He tells parables about the seed in the ground giving different yields, and the wheat and the weeds growing together. The same patterning is apparent in the Old Testament's progression from books on the Law to Wisdom literature. The crucial transition from Law to Wisdom passes through the Prophets.

While we find churches with many varieties of names throughout the world there are very few – if any – dedicated to Jesus the Prophet. That is telling us something about how we seem reluctant to allow the discomfiting message of the prophets to enter our consciousness. One way has been to reduce the prophets to the role of soothsayers, simply there to predict the coming of the Messiah. Their message is really about how to live now. Jesus clearly saw himself in the tradition of the Jewish prophets; he was well aware how the teachers of the Law were just as concerned to kill him as their forefathers had killed the prophets before him.

Sometimes, Catholics seem to think that Jesus came to start a new religion – Christianity, particularly its Catholic version. What he seems to be doing is trying to reform his own religion of Judaism, and in that way he is warning us against the tendency of ALL religion to keep us at an immature level of spiritual development. Ken Wilber says that religion has two important tasks to fulfil. The first one is to create the container for the first-half of life: to give us through tradition, customs, law and order, a sense of belonging, boundaries and a strong ego-identity. The second task is the shattering of that ego-identity so that we can move beyond our small (false) self to our God-self *(true-self)*. It is the move from ego-centric to soul-centric living. It allows us to move from the small picture to the bigger picture. It allows us to taste the wine.

This pattern of spiritual development is reflected in the biblical framing of the journey from Law through Prophets to Wisdom which represents *Order*, *Criticism* and *Integration*, and I am suggesting that Don Bosco's path of *Reason*, *Religion* and *Loving-kindness* fits a similar pattern. I am suggesting that the role of mature religion is to help us to get from the agenda for the first-half of life to the second, which is nothing other than transformation into a Christ-centred life saturated by compassion, mercy, forgiveness, love, what the people of Israel called *hesed.* The paradox is that we only truly honour and respect the journey of the first-half of life by growing away from it. This growing is not a rejection of what we have learned but a *true integration.* Jesus leads us into this when he says:

> Do not imagine that I have come to abolish the Law or the Prophets. I have come not to abolish but to complete. I tell you solemnly, till heaven and earth disappear, not one dot, not one little stroke, shall disappear from the Law until its purpose is achieved.[12]

Then we find Jesus saying, *You have heard it said of old...but I say to you.* This kind of coincidence of opposites is classic Wisdom teaching, so we need to ask, *What is the purpose of the Law that Jesus alludes to*? The answer is that the purpose of the Law is to get us to the point where we realise that we cannot keep it! This is the great defeat of the ego, and our ego doesn't like it one little bit, which is why we resist the second-half-of-life agenda. It is indeed a narrow gate, but one that leads to abundant life. It is precisely this reality that the prophets, one after the other, point out.

The first thing the prophets reveal is the essentially tragic nature of human life. Life is not fair. Even though we try to please God and keep the commandments, life is still not fair. God's promises of protection don't seem to work. People we know and love get sick and die. Young children get cancer or are born with physical or mental handicaps. Earthquakes, tsunamis, tornadoes, droughts all happen and seem to be beyond our control. The moral absolutes of the first-half of life don't seem to fit. On quite a few occasions when I have been preaching retreats, Catholic parents have come up to me to tell me that they have a son who is gay or a daughter who is a lesbian, or a daughter who is pregnant and having an abortion. Many today experience the breakup of their marriage and find themselves barred from communion. All of these happenings involve some form of suffering, which means some

12 Mt 5:17-18

kind of experience that I cannot control or fix. Something is happening to us and we don't know where God is in the midst of it all. The ego hates to lose control.

Such crises are in fact the gateway, the transition point, to the second-half of life. This goes to the heart of religion. How can religion help us deal with the reality of pain and suffering? Healthy religion teaches us that if we do not transform our pain, we will transmit it. All suffering tests our belief in a good, benevolent God. We will see later in this chapter how trying to discern his vocational path led Don Bosco to a serious breakdown when he was driven to the edge of his resources, in his early years as a priest. His trust in God wasn't broken and he was able to move through the crisis strengthened by grace.

Some people may be fortunate to have good health throughout most of their lives, but there is also a form of suffering none of us can escape. It is the experience of moral failure. However hard we try, we find that we cannot keep the Law perfectly. From time to time we all fail. I don't think there is anyone who can escape the harsh reality that for all our religious observances, our prayers, our attendance at Mass, our retreats, our good resolutions, we cannot escape the trap of judging others. All great religions teach the same, *Do not judge!* Yet we all fail. What is this telling us? That the ego that we built up in the first-half of life has to die as we move from egocentric religion to soul-centric spirituality, or as we Christians would say, Christ-centred living.

It is the shift from *will-power* to *willingness*. Richard Rohr has said that the greatest failure of institutional Christianity is its failing to guide us through this crisis into the second-half of life. If we cannot make this breakthrough we just go back to doing the first-half of life over and over again. Sadly, we see many Christians who are very observant, attend Mass, say prayers, appear to live good lives and yet are rigid, judgmental and, frankly, not very nice people to be with.

None of us is perfect or capable of perfection, and I think it is true that all of us have some kind of weakness that never goes away. Despite all our efforts and will-power we can't remove this wound. It is what Paul famously identified as *a thorn in the flesh*. It is at this point that we need wise guides, or elders, who can reassure us and reveal the heart of the good news: that this is the place where we meet a different God, not a God who wants to punish us for our failures. As our heroic moral egos meet failure, healthy religion invites us to surrender into the arms of a loving, forgiving, merciful God. Our wound becomes our gift; it becomes a sacred wound that we can take with us into the second-half of life. This is religion as transformation, and this is where the spiritual journey asks different questions. It is when we begin to discern what Jung called *what is really right from what is really wrong.*

The second-half of life brings the gift of wisdom and discernment, but it comes with a cost to the ego. We remain wounded, and we learn that the spiritual journey is not about effort and will-power so much as allowing God to work through us and in us, through our very brokenness. It is the shift from religion as performance, to religion as relationship which is a very Salesian direction. The scriptures show us that even in those first books of the bible that stress the importance of the Law, the wisdom of the wound was already known. In chapter 32 of Genesis we have the extraordinary account of Jacob, wrestling all night with a stranger. Was it a man, or an angel, or even God? Wrestling is a powerful image of the struggles of the soul. Even though Jacob did not submit, he has to pay a price. He is wounded at the hip and walks away limping from the encounter. In return, he asks for and is given a blessing. He is blessed in his brokenness, and the experience is so deep and profound that he says that he has seen the face of God and lived, and so becomes the father of the people with the name Israel.

Don Bosco's Crisis

When we consider the lives of our Salesian founders, Don Bosco and Mary Mazzarello, we can see a similar pattern. As they tried to discern the vocational direction of their lives they both experienced a severe crisis in their health.

With Don Bosco there is the danger of romanticising the famous dream at the age of nine. In his Memoirs of the Oratory he records for us his struggles with this dream which originally left him in tears asking the two noble figures, *who are you to demand the impossible of me?* He struggled for some years with the question of his vocation. He seemed quite nervous about becoming a priest, referring to some habits of the heart and lack of virtue. We might dismiss this as the false humility of the saint, but he correctly identified his struggles with his ego and his pride taking excessive pleasure in his ability with games, magic tricks, and other amusements. This is the self-critical thinking of the prophets.

The Lady in the dream had advised him *make yourself humble*, but shortly after his ordination he recalled travelling to give a sermon where he expected to be showered with praise, when instead he experienced a Pauline kind of humiliation. He was thrown off his horse and it taught him a severe lesson in humility and he resolved to preach in future to please God rather than impress his listeners with his erudition and cleverness. He even decided to give up all his athletic skills with games, but fortunately realised later that grace builds on nature and God had given him these gifts to use in his ministry.

After his ordination he continued to struggle with his vocational direction and even when he met poor and abandoned youngsters at the church of St Francis of Assisi he wasn't sure how to organise and develop this new kind of priestly work. In those years of the 1840s he thought of joining first the Franciscans, and then the Oblates with the idea of becoming a missionary. He finally ended up at the Refuge with Don Borel as a chaplain to young handicapped girls aged 3-13. This post seems to be taking him further away from his poor boys and his weekend Oratory gatherings. But with help from Don Borel and the Marchesa di Barolo he was able to continue for a time. But from 1844-1846 he was sent from pillar to post with his youngsters and it was a real time of crisis and suffering for Don Bosco. On what appeared to be his last day at the Oratory, he seemed very close to breakdown. In his Memoirs he describes his spirit as deeply troubled and worried, very disturbed; his energy is spent and his health was suffering. Walking alone he begins to cry as he begs God to help him. It is at that moment when he is led to meet Francis Pinardi whose rather ramshackle shed provided the home he needed for his poor boys.

The cost of all this uncertainty, however, was severe and at the point of exhaustion his health broke down in 1846. He was given the Last Rites and was ready to die. However, nursed back to health at home by his mother, he gradually recovered and returned with her on November 3rd 1846. In the judgement of Don Rua, that date marks the real beginning of the Salesian mission.[13]

Those years of struggle and suffering had led him to the edge of his resources and when he returns to his mission for his boys he has complete trust that this is what God wants him to do. He was fully launched on the second journey in which he dedicated all his energies to teaching and educating the young in the family spirit of loving-kindness.

Mary Mazzarello's Crisis

It is interesting to see a similar pattern in the life of Mary Mazzarello. She also went through a near-death experience, at the age of twenty one, when she contracted typhoid. Confined to bed for almost two months she was so close to death that her funeral was being arranged. Like Don Bosco she received the Last Rites and was ready to die. But also like Don Bosco she recovered and the experience seemed to lead her to re-evaluate her life. She could no longer engage with the same energy in her family farm. A new vocational path opened up for her, guided like Don Bosco, with a dream vision.

> Shortly after my illness, while I was standing on the hill of Borgo Alto I saw a large building in the exact spot where there had been only a hovel. I thought I was dreaming. What is this, I thought, I have never seen this before. When I looked into the building, I saw a number of young women dressed as Sisters and a voice said to me, *I entrust them to you.*[14]

This event awakened a desire that had previously been in her heart when at the age of fifteen she had been a member of the Daughters of Mary Immaculate. She now devoted herself to the guidance of young girls at Mornese and when she later

---

13 For a fuller account see Ian Murdoch *Starting Again from Don Bosco* (Don Bosco Publications, Bolton 2009)

14 Quoted in *One Heart* (Unpublished resource book by John Hunt and Salesian Spirituality Team, UK)

met Don Bosco, she co-founded with him the Salesian work for young girls.

The Great Turnaround

The nature of the transition from first to second-half-of-life spirituality is often some experience of falling, of failure, of sickness, whether physical or moral. The symbolic wounding inflicted on Jacob has to be acknowledged by all of us. This is the genius of the prophets who move us from the moral certitudes, the dualisms, the black-and-white judgements, the spiritual progress mentality of the first-half of life when we have been given our boundaries and told we are special in God's eyes. This is all very useful and good, but the point of it all is to get us to the place of failure, of vulnerability, of weakness, of some kind of suffering which the ego cannot fix. Then we either enter more deeply into the mystery of life or return to our ego agenda.

The key to this next level of consciousness, this surrender, is to accept the self-critical thinking of the prophets. Instead of criticising and comparing others as less-favoured by God than ourselves, we learn the humility to let God give us new software so that we can get connected to the Great Mystery that Jesus calls the Kingdom of God. For this to happen, our hearts have to be enlarged so that we detach from the narrow self-centred agenda of the *false-self,* and draw life from a deeper source when we discover the Great Mystery to be a mystery of compassion, mercy and forgiveness.

This is not a reward for our perfect behaviour. In fact, the people in the Gospel who thought they were experts in keeping the Law totally failed to understand Jesus and were shocked by his willingness to welcome and dine with sinners of all kinds. When Don Bosco and Mary Mazzarello urged Salesians and Daughters of Mary, Help of Christians to channel their energies to the poor and abandoned, they were showing us how deeply they were aligned with the compassionate love of Jesus. What our two great founders teach is to live a spirituality of loving-kindness, not so much in the style of the spiritually rich helping of the poor, but a genuine mutual relationship of give-and-take, whereby we allow the poor to teach us.

Don Bosco was well aware of the outpouring of prayer that his illness provoked in his beloved boys. We know that Salesian spirituality is essentially relational, and there can be no genuine relationship that simply goes in one direction. Obviously, as educators, we have much to give and offer to poor and abandoned youth. At the same time, we must never forget that the poor and abandoned youth keep our Salesian feet close to the spiritual fire.

To return to Fr Viganò's call to live Salesian spirituality in our times, I think we can say that the journey from the first-half of life to the second is a shift from religion as morality to a spirituality of mysticism as Karl Rahner envisaged. This does not mean that we abandon the Law because all authentic growth from dualistic black-and-white thinking to the non-dualism of unitive thinking has to both *transcend* and *include.* This is the enlargement of heart which so characterised both Don Bosco and Mary Mazzarello.

To *transcend* and *include* is to get closer to the path of Jesus who seemed to have little problem with sinners. This is the great turnaround of the Gospel. Many Christians still struggle with this, how Jesus seems to forgive and show compassion to all kinds of sinners. *We have to discover the Law is in fact a necessary stumbling block in the spiritual journey.* This was brilliantly pointed out by the prophet Isaiah:

> God is both sanctuary and stumbling stone, Yahweh is a rock that brings Israel down, the Lord is a trap and snare for the people.[15]

It seems that unless we fall, unless we are humbled, unless we are lost we can never be truly found.

The Importance of Mirroring

We can ask the question, how can we as adults help our young people to face this transition point later in their lives? For us, I think it is largely a question of mirroring. The word *mentoring* is often used today and it is a good one, but I think that mirroring goes to a much deeper more personal level. It is like fathering and mothering. Don Bosco was drawn to

15 Is 8:14

the young who were abandoned, those who had not been sufficiently loved by the mothers and fathers. Having lost his own father he was fortunate to have a wonderful and saintly mother to show him both unconditional and conditional love. He also benefited greatly from the wise guidance and affection of the saintly Don Cafasso who guided him away from the rigidities of Jansenism and the rather unbalanced obsessions of his friend Comollo. With Mary Mazzarello it was different. Her mirroring seems to have been given to her more by her father than her mother.

I think that mirroring is at the heart of the Salesian charism. It is personal and relational. We are called to be signs and bearers of God's special love for the young. In a world of broken families this kind of mirroring by a mature adult is needed more than ever and it is the best way to prepare our young people for the challenges that life will put before them as it unfolds into the second-half of life territory. It is essential if we are to discover a God who seems to prefer an intimate relationship to moral correctness. As we shall see, a profound mirroring encounter with God is at the heart of a more contemplative spirituality.

Chapter 3 – The Second-Half of Life

How can it be that a Salesian
has more important concerns than God?[16]

The purpose of healthy religion is to help us build a solid container, a good foundation for the task within the task that lies ahead. It starts with a good moral framework, a sense of right and wrong, good social skills, a healthy ego, an education that helps us to grow up, to work hard, to have a sense of identity, to be patriotic, to be proud of one's own roots. As life unfolds, however, we begin to experience more of the tragic nature of human life. We don't plan this, it just happens. We encounter paradoxes and contradictions, situations that don't easily fit into black-and-white absolutes. We meet suffering. This can happen very early with some young children, but generally it is a gradual dawning that we cannot control every aspect of our lives. We are not the centre of the universe.

This is the reality that the prophets point to and in doing so they uncover the true purpose of the Law, which is to get us into the boxing-ring, as it were, to give us something to cut our teeth on, to help us to really grow up, spiritually. The paradox is that this cannot happen without some kind of dying to the small self. This usually involves some experience of weakness, of failure, a wounding, that brings us to the edge of our resources. It can be a crisis of a near-death experience such as Don Bosco or Mary Mazzarello experienced, or it can be a moral *death* when we realise that we are not perfect, nor is anyone else, nor the world in which we live. Everything is caught up in the mystery of life that we call the Paschal Mystery. Reality is the greatest teacher in the spiritual journey. In the first-half of life we try to fit everything into our own point of view; in the second-half of life we are shaped by what is real, somewhere perhaps that, like Peter, we would rather not go.

We naturally fear this moment because none of us wants to die, and this is where healthy religion leads us to discover the real purpose of our lives, which is not to live inside the cocoon of our small selves but to discover our true selves which are

16 Fr Pascual Chávez *Acts of the General Council* (July – Sept 2003) p23

hidden with Christ in God. Initially, our small egos protect us from harm and danger. This is essentially defensive and protective work and it reinforces our egocentric world. Wisdom teaching on the other hand summons us to embark on the adventure of finding our true identity and purpose and it always involves some kind of wounding.

It is striking to see this kind of wisdom in classical literature and fairy tales. Many of them tell of a hero or heroine who may be a prince or princess, or even of divine origin, and yet are unaware of who they really are. They are summoned to leave the comforting security of home to embark on a perilous journey. It is there that the wounding takes place and in the great crisis of transformation, which is done to us, the wound becomes sacred.

At this point the real task becomes clear. The hero or heroine has to move from the old life to fall into – and it always seems like a falling – a much deeper stream or river. This is what *finding* or *saving* your soul really means, when we discover the great flow of life which sustains everything; the Great Mystery, the Great River, the Great Compassion, the Great Forgiveness. It is always an enlargement of spirit and soul, never a narrowing. The transformed yet wounded hero or heroine returns home with a new wisdom for the younger generation. Not all religious believers go through this stage; some, even those of no religion, do.

It is our task as Salesian *elders* to lead our young people to the edge of this mystery. This is true parenting or teaching when we can point our young people beyond the agenda of the small protective self. Clarissa Pinkola Estes relates how at the age of seven she was walking with her mother who pointed out the local church. *Always stay in touch with the church,* she tells her daughter, *but remember this: beneath the church is The River. Never lose touch with The River.* This is the Great River of life and it is where mature religion should lead us. It leads us from performance-related religion to the experience of union. It is the River of Compassion, what Don Bosco called *loving-kindness.*

Water and Blood

The theme of flowing water is central to the wisdom tradition of the bible. It is the great metaphor for union, the symbol of God flowing out to us to invite us into unitive consciousness. In the very beginning we have the Spirit of God moving over the waters of creation. Then we have the parting of the Red Sea, Moses striking the rock, Joshua leading the people across the Jordan, John the Baptist pouring water over the people, thirsting for God experience. We have Jesus, who undergoes John's baptism, telling the woman at the well that he will give her living water that will well up from inside her, which is a powerful metaphor for inner God experience. We see water pouring from the side of Jesus on Calvary, and the concluding words of the book of Revelation relate how the thirsty are invited to drink the water of life which is freely given at the conclusion of the whole biblical narrative.

We will examine the Trinitarian flow of life and love in a later chapter but it is enough to record here the evidence also of mystics such as Mechtild of Magdeburg, Julian of Norwich, Teresa of Avila and many others who use this kind of language. What is important to note is that some kind of inner experience of God is central to the second-half of life journey.

I am suggesting that spiritual life is meant to lead to a transformative journey, but it is not easy. It takes us away from our familiar comfort zones. That is why a second powerful code word is often used in the bible, and this is *blood*. It is blood that flows out of the side of Jesus alongside water on Calvary. This is the great transformative image of the death of the *false-self,* of our illusions, our addictions, even our reputation. It is a painful and challenging symbol.

The bible contains so many references to *blood sacrifices* and I think this has misled us into thinking that God demands blood from us if he is to be placated for our faults and forgive our sins. At the time of Jesus the main occupation of priests in the temple was the organising and killing of sacrificial animals. We have almost all been taught that God demanded a hideous blood sacrifice from Jesus. This is the dualistic mind at work. We seem to think that God is like us and wants revenge and punishment for those who offend him. I think it is very difficult to fall in love with such a God. Jesus reveals a very different kind of God, a God of mercy, forgiveness, and compassion, the loving-kindness of Don Bosco's Preventive System. This is the God we are invited to fall in love with in the second-half of life, not a God who demands the shedding of blood so that he will like us and forgive us. Instead of demanding blood sacrifices from us, Jesus reverses the whole direction of religion by shedding his blood to get to us.[17]

When Jesus overturns the money tables in the temple he is overthrowing the whole sacrificial system of bloodletting. For Jesus – and of course, his followers – the sacrifice is about giving up our own agenda and allowing the Father's will to flow through us.

> When Christ came into the world, he said, *Sacrifices and offerings you have not desired, but a body you have prepared for me, in burnt offerings and sin offerings you have taken no pleasure.* Then I said, *See, O God. I have come to do your will.*[18]

For Don Bosco, the whole notion of obedience is central and it seems to be the guiding principle of Salesian vowed life, but we will discuss this later.

From Certainty into Mystery

We have seen how the first-half of life lays the foundation for the future adventure. It is what all institutions have to do to get us started. We need some certainties and beliefs to hang on to, some clear moral choices. The Church tends to concentrate on this part of the journey. Today in our very bewildering world it is not surprising that the Vatican has spent a lot of time and energy reorganising the language of the liturgy. It seems to be part of a gradual pulling back from the excitement of Vatican II and many liberals are unhappy with this. In a sense it was almost inevitable that this would happen after Vatican II and we shouldn't be too surprised. It's what institutions do. They are by nature conservative, and the more complicated the bigger picture becomes, the more they turn towards micro management. Many clergy seem to operate as micro-managers, strong on control and keeping the rules,

17 Rene Girard *I See Satan Fall Like Lightning* (Orbis Books, NY 2001)
18 Heb 10:5-7

rather than wise elders who invite us to take the real risks of a faith-filled journey into mystery.

The second-half of life calls for the surrender of control. Perhaps religious leaders have, at times, preferred power, prestige and control rather than the humble leadership of Jesus. Recent scandals in the Church are revealing this misuse of power. It is interesting to see how Don Bosco refused to accept the title of *Monsignor* because he did not want to create any distance between himself and his boys. For Don Bosco, relationships were far more important than any clerical privileges. That is second-half-of-life spirituality. Jesus does this all the time. He is far more interested in people's relationship with him than tests of doctrinal orthodoxy. For him, it was always about orthopraxis, *by their fruits you shall know them.* Too much head-knowledge can lead to pride and arrogance. Those who know God are always humble before the mystery. Jesus himself used parables to describe the new consciousness that he called *The kingdom of God.* He never defined it; he simply said, *It is like this, it is like that.*

Inner Experience

The mystics suggest that the most authentic language for the Great Mystery that we call God, is silence. Silence provides a more spacious place in which to receive the mystery of life, not to be overcome by inconsistencies and imperfection, both in ourselves and others. We are given the grace to move beyond the simple certainties and judgements of the first-half of life when we like to make distinctions between what is right and what is wrong. We use our reason to analyse, to sort out the good guys from the bad guys. We like law and order, when the good get rewarded for keeping the rules and the bad get punished. Jesus seemed to pursue a very different agenda: he met with, dined with, and welcomed sinners; he reached out to foreigners, he praised Samaritans, publicans, women and tax collectors who sought his presence. He touched lepers and healed Romans. He claimed that a sinful publican was closer to God than a proud law-abiding Pharisee. Not surprisingly he met strong opposition from the religious officials and leaders who thought they understood the Law.

> All the tax-collectors and sinners were coming near to listen to him. And the pharisees and scribes were grumbling and saying, *This fellow welcomes sinners and eats with them.*[19]

Jesus just wants to push his listeners into second-half of life religion, beyond basic law-abiding performance into non-duality, which is another word for wisdom that can hold opposites together rather than exclude the part we don't like:

> You have heard that it was said, *You shall love your neighbour and hate your enemy.* But I say to you, *Love your enemies and pray for those who persecute you so that you may be children of your Father in heaven; for he makes his sun to rise on the evil and the good and sends his rain on the righteous and the unrighteous.*[20]

If we are honest, I think we have to admit that we rarely do this. Christians that do this tend to stand out. It cannot be done by the simplistic judgments and the clarity of the first-half of life. It brings us squarely into the self-critical thinking of the prophets. It teaches us to hold the tension inside ourselves rather than seek to pin the blame on another. Of course we have to make judgements; but we learn to say *Yes* before we say *No.* Remember Don Bosco's warning never to correct a young person when we are angry.

Shadow Work

For this to become possible we have to pay attention to what the prophets taught, what modern psychology calls *shadow work.* This is essential for everyone, but I think it is vital for spiritual leaders such as clergy and religious. We have all been given a role as official religious teachers, especially the clergy. This is a *persona*, a kind of mask that we wear before others. The role demands that we are experts in the things of the spirit, but we must also remain connected with and grounded in our souls. This is truly *incarnational religion* when the spirit that wants to soar to the heavens is united with the soul that keeps us rooted in the real and mundane. It is not that, without a good *spirit/soul* balance, we will fall like Icarus, who flew too close to the sun. We will inevitably

19 Lk 15:1-2
20 Mt 5:43-45

fall, because the fall is the necessary humbling experience, the narrow gate through which we enter the second-half of life. As Thomas More says the issue is not, *Will I crash as a result of my spiritual ambitions and explorations*, but *How and when will I fall?*

Jesus is well aware of this necessary stumbling stone when at the end of the Beatitudes he says:

> Blessed are you when people revile you and persecute you and utter all kinds of evil against you falsely on my account. Rejoice and be glad.[21]

This is aimed at my *false-self* that wants everybody to tell me how good and wonderful I am. The saints and mystics don't really have an *I* to protect. They have gone beyond that to live in conscious union with the *I AM* of God. The *true-self* has nothing to protect or worry about. This is the freedom of the second-half of life. The closer we get to the light the greater the shadow, which is why truly holy people are always humble. Denial of this shadow lay behind much of the damaging cover-ups by Church leaders, confronted with the reality of sexual abuse.

Whenever you are upset, or have a strong emotional reaction your shadow has been touched and, this will always occur, to a degree, even in the lives of the saints. Living in conscious union allows us to hold together the opposites of light and dark in creative tension. We are always a mixture of saint and sinner, light and dark, good and bad. If we are not prepared to recognise this, what usually happens is that we push the shadow, our dark side, onto somebody else. The transition to the second-half of life allows us to live not in anger at our frailties, but to embrace them with compassion, forgiveness and loving-kindness.

From Fear to Friendship

Even though Don Bosco was brought up in a climate of Jansenism, which took a very restrictive view of God's love, he was able to move beyond it and steer his boys into a much more serene and affectionate spirituality. His teaching on

21 Mt 5:11-12

loving-kindness is rooted in a very attractive image of God as a loving Father. He placed friendship and cheerfulness at the core of his spirituality. Young people of all ages want to grow up and live happy lives. Don Bosco created a whole climate and atmosphere in his Oratory so that the young would feel welcomed, at home, free to make friends and be happy. He used music, theatre, games, and all these gifts of nature were nurtured by a strong religious faith – healthy religion, in other words.

This wasn't always easy for Don Bosco because in his time of formation the climate of Jansenism was still pervasive, as Ian Murdoch points out:

> Understandings of Christian and priestly life and spirituality at the seminary in Chieri in the 1830s left a lot to be desired. The emphasis was on flight from the world, upon death, judgement and the question of predestination, a sense of sin that restricted sacramental life, fostered excessive penance and mortification, and cast a pall of gloom over the spiritual life.[22]

There are still some aspects of this in his later spirituality, in the emphasis on saving one's individual soul, for example. But, more than anything, Don Bosco wanted to offer his boys a religion of loving-kindness and friendship. His youngsters clearly often idolised him and it is this personal attraction, this personal relationship, that he was able to create with so many of them that is so striking. He gave them a strong grounding in religious belief and practice that would be the ideal preparation for what might happen in later life. In *The Companion of Youth* he wrote, *Train a child in the way he should go and even when he is old he will not depart from it.*[23]

As Salesians today, in a very different world from Don Bosco, we face the same challenge and the warning of Fr Chávez about the heresy of activism is especially relevant here. In western culture much of the traditional support system of a shared faith-culture has gone. Family life, too, has changed dramatically. Rather than make us lose faith in our Salesian approach, I think it should strengthen it. Our model for

22 Ian Murdoch *Starting Again from Don Bosco* (Don Bosco Publications, Bolton 2009) p88
23 *The Companion of Youth (Il Giovane provveduto)* 1847

evangelisation has to be friendship. If we find ourselves, as Salesians, caught up in a workaholic lifestyle I would suggest it is covering over an inability to relate at any depth, not just with other people but also with God.

In the Western World, in recent years, the number of vocations to religious life has fallen considerably. I have written elsewhere[24] about religious life as a liminal form of life. That means it is a call to live the deepest values in a culture. I think that second-half of life spirituality is a good way to do this, with friendship very much at the heart of it. Young people today are caught between a secular climate that tells them that anything goes in the area of sexual behaviour and a Church that still struggles to present a healthy and positive view of sexuality.

It is not a question of abandoning the first-half-of-life agenda. It is about transcending it. When you move to a higher level of consciousness in the spiritual life it should always be a case of *transcend* and *include*. In the dualistic religion of the past, this did not often happen. In fact, dualism is a strong sign of low-level religious development. The Protestant Reformation is a classic case in point. It was pure *either/or* thinking. We are right, we have the right formulae, the right words, the right container, and we are so convinced we are right that we will torture you and kill you for disagreeing. Both sides, Catholic and Protestant, did this, and it highlights a crucial element in the revival of a more contemplative spirituality in the world today. It is the problem of the thinking, egocentric mind and it is this issue that contemplation addresses.

---

24 Michael Cunningham *Within & Without* (Don Bosco Publications Bolton 2003)

Chapter 4 – Discovering an Inclusive Tradition

> What I could continually perceive was his constant union with God. He manifested these sentiments of love of God with such spontaneity that we could see that they sprang from a mind and heart that were always immersed in the contemplation of God.[25]

These words of Michael Rua, Don Bosco's closest collaborator and first successor, are echoed by other superiors who knew Don Bosco personally. Fr Paul Albera testified to his constant union with God and Fr Philip Rinaldi was strongly convinced that Don Bosco was continually united to God in prayer. Despite these statements by those authoritative figures who lived with him, many Salesians have formed the view that Don Bosco was just a man of action. He was, indeed, highly active, but there can be no doubt that he lived a life of real intimacy with God. But he didn't teach contemplative prayer to his followers. In our Salesian history there has been little, if any, evidence of any systematic teaching of contemplative prayer to young Salesians in formation programmes. I can't recall any in my own years of formation. In my experience of preaching retreats in many parts of the Western World, I would suggest this is true for many religious congregations and seminaries. I don't think there is any doubt that Don Bosco had a deep and intimate inner prayer life, but he didn't teach anything other than discursive meditation, which is of course praying with words, concepts and images.

Don Bosco was a man of his time. Fr Chávez has pointed out that his knowledge and use of scripture reflected that of his times. The same is true, I suggest, of his teaching on prayer. There have always been two types of prayer in the Church: *cataphatic* and *apophatic*. They are not very user-friendly words but they are the best we have. Cataphatic Prayer (sometimes spelled with a *k*) involves praying with words and images and includes prayers such as vocal prayer, liturgical prayer, the Prayer of the Church, devotional prayer, the rosary

25 Blessed Michael Rua Quoted in Alois Kothgasser SDB, *The Little Window of the Valponasca* (Don Bosco Publications, New Rochelle 1982) p152

and discursive meditation. *Apophatic* means to go beyond all words, concepts and images into silence. In Don Bosco's time the teaching and practice of silent prayer, or contemplative prayer as it is called, had virtually died out in the Western Church. A rich tradition was almost lost.

Sometimes I hear Salesians say that contemplative prayer is not really part of our tradition. In a narrow sense I think this is true, but the judgement rests on what I would consider a very limited understanding of the word *tradition.* Healthy tradition needs to remain open to both the past and the present, otherwise there is a danger that we cut ourselves off from some deep and vital resources for the spiritual journey. Taking Fr Viganò's reminder that *we are with Don Bosco and the times not with the times of Don Bosco* we have to be open to continued enrichment of tradition by keeping it available to the promptings of the Holy Spirit. Jesus himself said that there were many more things that he wanted to tell his disciples but they were not ready for them: that would be the unfolding task of the Spirit. Today there is growing evidence that the Holy Spirit is inviting many people, not just religious and priests, but many lay people into a more contemplative way of praying.

Any authentic Christian tradition has to go back to the Jesus of the Gospels. Today we are discovering that he was probably the first non-dual teacher in the West. The problem with the dualistic mind which has dominated Western thinking is its inherent tendency to divide the field, to see reality as *either/or,* black-and-white, good and bad. This may be fine for the first-half of life – the largely moral agenda we looked at earlier – but as we grow in the spiritual journey, a different way of seeing and understanding is needed. I think it is true to say that most Christians still see Jesus as a divine but not fully human figure, despite the *both/and* teaching of the Council of Nicea. In the mystery of the Incarnation Jesus shows us how to put the human and the divine together, but the dualistic mind struggles to embrace this paradoxical truth. The whole point of the Incarnation was the overcoming of this divide. Christianity proclaims the union of divinity and humanity, but we still find it difficult to get our heads round this amazing fact. It seems as if we are using the wrong software and dualism will not get us there however hard we work for God.

In the dualistic mind, we convince ourselves that we are human beings and our task is to become *spiritual*. We feel that we are always separate from God and religion is the means to get ourselves saved or into heaven, and this is the religion of the first-half of life. It is all about correct beliefs, good behaviour, attendance at Mass, saying prayers and working as hard as we can. Sadly this doesn't seem to transform many Christians into living like *new creations* as Paul would say. Jesus invites us to live life at a new level of consciousness, one that can hold together the great paradoxes that go beyond the dualistic mind: to accept that Jesus is fully divine and that he is also fully human, and that we are all invited into the mystery of participation called the Trinity. The step is from life as separation from God to life as participation in God's own life, from working for God to an intimate relationship. Clearly we are not God, but nor are we separate from God. This is what Jesus means when he says *stay connected to the vine*, outside of which our efforts will not bear fruit. If our life is reduced to mere activism in the strong words of the Rector Major, there can be no authentic Salesian mission.

We need words, good psychology, good philosophy, good theology but they always come up against a ceiling. The saints and mystics understood this. We need a different software to deal with the great mysteries such as life and death, suffering, eternity and God. The dualistic mind tends to seize on what it can understand and to call it *truth*. What it can't understand is dismissed. This is the egocentric bloc in our Western culture. The role of mature religion and wisdom is to leave the door open to what I cannot understand. This openness to mystery is non-dual thinking and it is impossible without a good grounding in humility. Just because I don't understand something doesn't make it false. Humility may not be a popular virtue these days, but if we could only accept our smallness, our very ordinary life, we begin to participate in the Great Mystery, in the Great Compassion. In the biblical pattern of Incarnation God always seems to come disguised in littleness, in the ordinary, in the particular. He comes into the world as a helpless infant recognised only by lowly shepherds and by wise men. Here lies revealed the essential paradox in our humanity; here are the two halves of our souls: lowly shepherds and wise men. It is a blessed paradox and it holds the great truth that although we are insignificant on our own yet we are called to greatness in the mystery of participation that is God. When we can hold opposites together, a deeper truth can emerge. This is non-dual wisdom.

I don't think that we can really understand much of what Jesus is saying without some *non-dual* thinking. Two obvious examples from Matthew's Gospel are when he says in chapter five that his Father allows *the sun to rise on good and bad men alike and his rain to fall on the just and the unjust.*[26] In chapter thirteen he relates the parable of the wheat and the weeds, and when the servants want to pull out the weeds the owner says, *No, you might damage the wheat as well, so let them both grow together.*[27] This is classic second-half-of-life spirituality.

To live this in unitive consciousness is what Jesus means by prayer. It is what we mean by non-dual consciousness, or contemplation. The rediscovery of the contemplative mind today is helping us to see how we have too often restricted prayer to *saying prayers.* We had largely forgotten key aspects of what Jesus taught about prayer, by putting everything inside the cataphatic tradition; but that is only one half of what Jesus taught. He told us not to babble on like the pagans, and he told us *to go into our inner rooms and close the door.* I suspect that for around ninety per cent of Christians – and this includes priests and sisters – prayer means saying prayers. You can say prayers all day with a dualistic mind. We have to find a way to stop the thinking mind. You get hints of it when people speak about thinking outside the box. There has to be some way to go beyond the normal mind-set with its built-in prejudices rooted inevitably in my own individualistic point of view.

The dualistic mind is not bad. It is necessary. It produces engineers, technicians, scientists, mathematicians; it produced the scientific and the industrial revolutions whose benefits we enjoy, but it can only get you so far in the encounter with mystery. Quantum physics is leading the way – going beyond

26 Mt 5:45

27 Mt 13:24-30

the ceiling, but it was always the task of healthy religion to honour but also go beyond the rational mind. Sadly, we Catholics have got so caught up in exclusionary thinking and proving that we are the best that we may be the most difficult institution to convince of the need to move to a new level of consciousness. We have tried to control God by telling him who he could love and who he could not love. Think for example of what we say about homosexuals. We have been like busy Martha, so caught up in our activity that we wanted to tell Jesus how to be God: *Tell my sister*. To be caught up in the dualistic mind, is to get trapped into judging others as not quite as good as we are.

Most people are called to the vocation of marriage and in the experience of falling in love with another person we are enlarged and taken into a bigger picture. This bigger field is the place that can include the dark side. Today we see so many relationships breaking up, once difficulties arise, and the romantic flush starts to fade. We are less able to deal with the dark side. In the Church we priests often get so caught up in our activities that our life of intimacy with the Lord suffers. Without that we cannot really guide and teach others who struggle with relational problems. We over-stress the moral issues while not leading people into the mystical journey that reveals the essential contradictions and paradoxes at the heart of the spiritual journey. You can meet many good Christians today and yet there is still the tendency to exclusionary thinking. Authentic love can break open this egotistic thinking and to experience such a love is to experience non-dual thinking, even though you may not call it that, because authentic love includes accepting the contradictions of the other person and learning to forgive them.

The Hidden Thread

Throughout Christian history the contemplative tradition has always been present but usually in a minor key, a sub-text to the main tradition of cataphatic spirituality. What is emerging today is the desire among many to bring this hidden tradition more into the mainstream. It is not just about praying, it is a way of seeing, a way of being, based more on transformation rather than simply formation. Formation is good and necessary and every religious congregation has its formation programmes; but few address the issue of transformation, and yet this is what Jesus was teaching. You see it in his two great one-liners which cannot be understood by the dualistic mind, *The Father and I are one*, and *whatever you do to the least of these brothers and sisters of mine you do to me.* This is classic non-dualism, but if we are honest, most Christians let it pass over their heads. Non-dual thinking doesn't divide the field, it doesn't eliminate the negative; it puts it all together.

Even the apostles, who lived with Jesus, found themselves lapsing into dualistic thinking and the Acts of the Apostles records the struggles of the Early Church leadership, including Peter, as they tried to fit Gentile converts into the old wineskins of Judaism. It was Paul who fought for an inclusionary solution and then Peter follows him when he makes one of the great non-dual statements of the scriptures: *Today I learned God has no favourites.* Sadly the dualistic mind took over again and by the end of the first century we Christians had rejected the Jewish people and tradition from which Jesus and Mary and all the apostles had emerged.

Non-dual thinking emerges again during the time of the desert fathers and mothers in the fourth century who just did what Jesus did: they told little stories and parables. On the surface they seem like simple stories, but they always subvert the ego like Jesus does when he says that the men who came at the last hour get paid just as much as those who laboured in the heat of the day. This breaks down our normal rational categories and many good Christians and good people today still resent the arrival of asylum seekers and immigrants on the grounds that there really isn't enough to go round. *We should come first*, they often say, *these foreigners should really go back to their own countries.*

The non-dual tradition was preserved in the second century by figures such as Clement of Alexandria who first used the word *mysticus* which means hidden, unsayable, that which cannot be put into words, and the influential figure of Origen. In the third century we find Plotinus, who building on Plato, created a whole philosophical understanding of consciousness, of Being and how everything is deeply connected to a world beyond the physical and the material. In the fourth century the towering figure of Augustine wrote his Confessions in the second person, addressing God in the most intimate language. He was so far ahead of his time.

In 313 AD when Constantine made Christianity the official religion of the empire it seemed to mark a great triumph, but in reality it allied religion with power and control. It is not surprising that this is when religious life begins to emerge. When the centre gets too powerful, some deeper thinkers want to go to the margins, and that is exactly what the desert fathers and mothers did in the fourth century. They kept the contemplative mind alive, and in their teaching they sought to imitate Jesus with those simple stories aimed at undermining the controlling power of the ego and the dualistic mind.

In the sixth century while St Benedict was creating monasteries and structures to keep religious life secure, figures like Pseudo-Dionysius were developing the apophatic tradition of prayer and spirituality. At its heart was the coincidence of opposites: that knowing must be balanced by unknowing, that certitude must be balanced by mystery, that words must be balanced by silence. All this subtlety was to be swept away at the Reformation when Christians killed and tortured each other in the name of Jesus, in the name of power, in the name of control.

Gradually the systematic teaching of a more contemplative spirituality was forced back into a few monasteries. The outstanding example here was the monastery of St Victor in Paris in the eleventh century and the figure of Hugh of St Victor, who taught how to go beyond the mind, to think without thinking. However, less and less of this teaching was available to the laity. The clergy thought it was beyond them; many still do today.

In the twelfth, thirteenth and fourteenth centuries there was an explosion of mysticism with Hildegard of Bingen, Francis and Clare, Mechtild of Magdeburg, Catherine of Siena, Richard Rolle and Julian of Norwich among others. Julian's writings were lost for centuries and have been rediscovered for our times. In the fourteenth century also, the Hesychasts influenced by Symeon, the new theologian, emerged in Greek Orthodox spirituality with their teachings on the inner life of prayer, but after the split between Rome and the Eastern Churches this tradition was lost to the West. A teacher in a Salesian school recently told me how he attended long and leisurely liturgies during a holiday in Greece, something that we in the West would find very challenging!

The Protestant Reformation and the Enlightenment mark the high point of dualistic teaching, introducing the period that Owen Barfield calls *the desert of non-participation.* In a sense, both had to happen and in our more tolerant times the ecumenical movement is struggling, not without difficulty, to achieve a more *both/and* approach to different views. The Enlightenment was also necessary and we know that the first pillar of Don Bosco's Preventive System is reason. To move to a higher level of consciousness, to move from a divided field to a unified field, to the second-half of life agenda, we have to *tanscend* and include. The problem with the Enlightenment was that reason was seen as giving access to all knowledge. But in responding to the critique of reason the Church drew a veil over its rich mystical tradition and fought back with our own rationalistic mind.

During the last four hundred years or so we have been living in this desert of non-participation. The mystical tradition, however, never died out. Even in the years of the Reformation we had those towering figures in the Carmelite tradition: Teresa of Avila and John of the Cross. In the seventeenth century Jean-Pierre de Caussade emerged as the Eckhart Tolle of his day, writing about the sacrament of the present moment, or what Tolle calls the *power of now.* And we have our own patron, Francis of Sales.

The twentieth century marks the real rediscovery of the mystery of participation with figures such as Therese of Lisieux, Evelyn Underhill, Bede Griffiths, Elisabeth of the Trinity, Martin Luther King, Simone Weil, Anthony de Mello, and Thomas Merton who perhaps more than any other figure in our time pulled back the veil as it were and rediscovered the contemplative riches of the Western tradition. It is interesting to note that Merton wasn't initially popular among his own

Cistercian community because he told them that they weren't contemplatives, but just *saying prayers.* Because of Merton there has been an explosion of interest in contemplation today led by teachers such as Thomas Keating, John Main, Ken Wilber, Karl Rahner, Gerald May, Cynthia Bourgeault, Ruth Burrows, James Finlay and Eckhart Tolle, among many others. There are many other figures who could be mentioned and we must not forget the other religions such as Judaism, Islam – the mystic Rumi is said to be the most widely read poet in the world today – Hinduism and Buddhism which have kept the mystical core of religion alive.

What is emerging in our times is a profound shift in our understanding of the spiritual journey from an isolated struggle for personal salvation to a shared journey of transformation. We are rediscovering the importance of practices to help us to do this. This rediscovery calls for a new understanding of tradition, a shift from an exclusionary view to an inclusive one. If the quantum physicists are revealing the deep connection of all things, this insight refers to every aspect of our humanity. Both Don Bosco and Francis of Sales lived in those difficult Post-Reformation times when Catholics and Protestants were still largely antagonistic to each other. Today I am sure they would be challenging us to embrace a more inclusionary spirituality. Mature religion is leading us into the second-half of life agenda by inviting us beyond our small egocentric minds into this wider and bigger picture.

We have to be taught how to do this and I will look more closely at a method of centering prayer in the next chapter. It is important to stress that contemplation is not anti-mind. In our rationalistic age some would dismiss contemplation as pre-rational. Ken Wilber responds by saying it is not pre-rational but trans-rational. The rational enlightenment was a devastating attack on non-dual thinking and we in the Church fought back in the same rational mode, when we should have been pointing to the paradoxes at the heart of Great Mystery that cannot be comprehended by the rational mind alone.

Chapter 5 – Seeing with Heart and Mind

> And the Spirit immediately drove him out into the wilderness. He was in the wilderness for forty days, tempted by Satan: and he was with the wild beasts and the angels waited on him.[28]

Our Western minds love method and technique. When we are challenged to do something new and different, our first question is often, *How do I do it?* We don't like too much introspection, we prefer to get on with things. Invited to pray in a contemplative way, we naturally want to know about method. I have been trying to suggest in this book that contemplation is not just a different way of praying; it is a different way of seeing reality. There has been a growth and interest in meditation in recent years, even in business circles. It is valued as a way of reducing stress which, given the general driven-quality of modern life, is such a problem for so many. A CEO had been encouraging his workforce to meditate for a few minutes each day. Meeting a busy young manager, he asked him if he were able to do this for fifteen minutes a day. The man replied that he was far too busy. *Then do it for thirty minutes,* was the response. This kind of therapeutic dimension of *silent prayer/meditation* has been gaining ground even as a means of gaining some control over many of our knee-jerk reactions to events and to people.

When the Spirit drove Jesus into the wilderness, I don't think it was to relieve his stress levels, even though that is no bad thing in itself. Tradition tells us that Jesus was around thirty years of age when he began his public ministry so it raises the question, *Why did he have to make a long and silent retreat after he was baptised by John?* It appears that he wanted to be truly centred, to really absorb that declaration that he was the beloved Son of the Father. We have no inside knowledge of Jesus' consciousness of who he was but it seems that he gives us an important lesson in making the inner journey: that all his loving deeds of forgiveness and compassion would flow out from this foundational relationship with his Father. He always

28 Mk 1:12-13

described his mission as doing the work of his Father. The desert was the place of under-stimulation; if it was important for Jesus to spend time there in his day, how much more does our highly-extraverted world require us to engage with the deeper level of our souls. I think this is very relevant for busy Salesians. A mature life is always about balance and harmony. As we will see later in the chapter, Don Bosco exhibited this calm and centered union with God in all his activity.

What is interesting today is that science is confirming that some form of *meditation/contemplation* does indeed reduce blood pressure and stress, it also helps us to deal with some of our more neurotic and knee-jerk responses to situations. Some people try this in order to control the mind and to experience stillness, a much-needed quality in our times. The story is told of a farmer looking over a fence when he sees a man clattering towards him on a speeding horse. He asks the man where he is heading. *No idea,* replies the rider, *Ask the horse!*

Recent findings by the HeartMath Institute[29] have uncovered very interesting information for those who take the spiritual journey seriously. Research is proving that *meditation/ contemplation* doesn't just help to reduce stress but, more importantly, it transforms and changes the way a person thinks. It is not about the content or what you think, but how you think. It changes the very way we see and perceive reality. This is very much needed for Christians today because the Church has spent a lot more time and energy in telling us what to think rather than how to think. The mystics have been much more concerned about how to think and that is why it is fascinating to see modern neuro-science reinforcing this ancient wisdom. What it does, in effect, is to re-wire the brain, by changing our neural pathways. This is exactly what spiritual teachers call non-dual consciousness. Whereas, in the past, this was attained by a few isolated mystics, non-dual consciousness is now appearing in many parts of the world.

I think this is a crucial reason for the rediscovery of contemplation in our time, because our world is going through a profound cultural shift. We seem to be coming to an end

29 www.heartmath.org

to what has been called the axial age which has enthroned reason as our primary way of dealing with reality. Our world is witnessing so many crises: the Western economies are in dire trouble, we see people rising up against repressive regimes asking for basic freedoms, many institutions are in crisis, many leaders seem uncertain what to do, we have riots and street demonstrations against rampant capitalism, we face an environmental crisis that many still deny, and threats from international terrorism. We are living through a time of profound transition and some are suggesting that a second axial age is beginning to emerge which will not reject reason but will move to a new level of consciousness that will *tanscend* and include, uniting both dualistic thinking and non-dual consciousness.

The year 2017 will mark five hundred years since Martin Luther nailed his ninety-five theses to the cathedral door in Wittenberg, the beginning of what we call the Protestant Reformation. To commemorate this event Catholics and Lutherans have set up a joint commission to examine the rights and wrong of both sides. This is a good example of non-dual thinking and a very constructive way of responding to a time of rampant dualism when both sides simply dug in and defended their positions, even to the point of being prepared to kill their opponents in the name of Jesus.

In recent years, biblical scholars have highlighted how the kingdom of God was at the heart of the life and teaching of Jesus. It was not a political vision, nor simply a place you go to after death. It is a reality to be experienced now, at its heart is a way of seeing. The kingdom of God implies a non-dual way of seeing reality. Kingdom consciousness cannot be earned; it is already given. It is something to become conscious of, to awaken into. It is characterised by abundance, generosity, mercy and compassion. Is it not about generating more action plans or moral crusades. It allows us to see people and creation as God sees them. This is the whole point of silent contemplative prayer and is central to the contemplative revival in Christianity. Instead of operating exclusively from egocentric minds we learn to put on what Paul calls *the mind of Christ*. If we are honest many of us don't want to do this; we prefer to live inside our own small minds.

There are different methods in contemplative prayer, but I want to concentrate on what is called *centering prayer.*[30] Whatever method gets you to meditate is good, so stay with it, but I think that centering prayer does have a unique approach I find very helpful. When we think about contemplative prayer we usually think of it as a way of stilling the mind. So a good prayer experience would be one in which we quiet the mind by some concentrative techniques. The clear goal is to still the mind. In fact this is impossible. Certainly in our highly extraverted culture it is very difficult and leads to the kind of failure that would make most people give up very quickly.

The goal of centering prayer is not to still the mind but to master the art of letting go. Whenever a thought, or indeed an emotion, captures our attention all we have to do is gently let it go. As a priest, I have listened to many people confessing distractions in prayer. I try to suggest that distractions are not sinful; they are inevitable, given the make-up of what the Buddhists aptly call our *monkey mind,* that just can't stop swinging from thought to thought. Thomas Keating, one of the founders of centering prayer, re-assured a woman who told him of her repeated failures to prevent thoughts flowing through her mind, that each distraction, provided a wonderful opportunity for an act of love. All we have to do when we become aware of a distraction is to return to loving attention in our prayer. So our thoughts are in fact tools for the journey that turn out to be our friends rather than our enemies.

Where some meditation methods recommend the use of a mantra which is repeated constantly during the session, in centering prayer all that is needed is one word which is used whenever we become aware of a distracting thought or emotion, this word is called your *sacred word.* Use it to return gently to that deeper part of your soul, your spiritual consciousness. It can be a word such as *love, peace, joy, Abba, Jesus,* or *Spirit.* As another distracting thought floats in, just let it go by returning to your sacred word. Just use your word to let go of this mental chatter.

It might seem pointless to keep doing this but in fact what

30 The spelling is American because this is where it originated

is happening is very helpful in the spiritual journey. Each act of letting go is uniting ourselves with a crucial part of the spiritual path lived by Jesus, which Paul calls *kenosis*, letting go. The more we think from our ordinary awareness, the more we experience ourselves as a separate egoic self. This is where most of us are trapped. When I meet someone I may reveal myself as a Salesian, a priest, a white male, an Englishman, a teacher, a writer, a lover of football and the music of the blues and so on. These characteristics reveal who I think I am by emphasising differences. In non-dual awareness or the contemplative mind, what matters most is not what differentiates me from others but what unites us: the gift of being, the I am, that we all receive from the Ground of all Being, that we call God. This brings about what spiritual teachers call unitive consciousness, what Jesus calls living inside the kingdom of God.

Regular daily practice of contemplative prayer of twenty minutes a day allows us to move out of our egoic identity with less fear and more confidence as we begin to feel more at home in our spiritual consciousness. We learn how to move to that deeper place where we may glimpse our *true-self* and learn to respect the *true-self* of others. This may be a very fleeting experience because we do not control our *true-self* and it is impossible to put into words. At the end of prayer time, it is important to attempt to evaluate our prayer session – that is what the ego wants to do. It is not about control, it is about surrender to the loving presence of God.

The Mind of Christ

The dualistic mind too easily dismisses contemplative prayer as an irrelevant distraction for busy, highly-motivated people. With a simple *either/or* it perpetuates the division in religious life between active and contemplative lives. The daily practice of contemplation changes this way of thinking and moves us to a more balanced *both/and* understanding. Gradually we begin to take on the mind of Christ which sees no contradiction at all between prayer and work, as is evident in Jesus's own life with his repeated withdrawals from ministry to spend time in prayer on his own, more often in nature rather than the synagogue.

This union of prayer and action is not achieved by moral striving, but by a shift in perception. Cynthia Bourgeault uses a useful contemporary metaphor to illustrate how this works. She compares it to installing a new operating system on a computer. Our normal everyday egoic operating system is fine for everyday tasks, but it simply cannot deal with the complexities of life, the mass of contradictions that we meet both in ourselves and others. It does a useful job for us in the first-half of life. We can't really grow up without our ego identity and the necessary boundaries it gives us.

The shift to the second-half of life agenda demands a new system because the egoic operating system sees the world through the eyes of the *false-self.* It is inherently anxious and fearful, and distrustful of others, because it sees the world through the image of scarcity. The *false-self* is trapped in concerns about what we have, what we do, and what others think of us. If mature religion does its job rightly it awakens us to a new operating system which is in fact our birthright. It has always been there, but only emerges with maturity. It allows us to move from simplistic black-and-white judgements to the bigger picture of compassion, forgiveness, mercy, our Salesian loving-kindness. It seems to take a while for most of us to become aware of it, as we face the challenges of the second-half of life. Mystical teachers refer to it as the heart and our modern scientific insights are confirming this. It is often called *the eye of the heart.*

Where the egocentric system looks out at the world from scarcity, differences, and fear, the heart perceives things as a whole. It's like looking through a stained glass window and seeing a picture of a saint rather than a series of coloured segments. It perceives through resonance and harmony. My *true-self* always wants to connect with the *true-self* of the Other. It is inherently relational, not in the sense of just connecting with people I like and approve of, but also to see the connection with people my ego doesn't like. I will explore more some aspects of Salesian relational spirituality in later chapters.

It has been suggested to me by some Salesians that a more contemplative spirituality is for the elite. I can understand why they say this because this is the way contemplation has been side-lined by mainline spirituality, but I don't think it is true because it creates a division between ordinary life and the spiritual life. If we are spiritual beings who have to learn how to become human, the emergence of a non-dual way of seeing is the natural unfolding of a mature consciousness. I agree with Gerald May when he says that *contemplation happens to everyone*. It happens when we are undefended, open and truly present. Presence is such a key word in Salesian spirituality.

The crises that afflict our planet these days are calling for this more unified way of seeing. I don't think it is an option; I think it is part of the evolutionary nature of our humanity. Sometimes we like to divide those we meet into head-people who live out of the left-brain of rational, analytical thinking, and heart-people who we say are more in touch with their emotions. When spiritual teachers speak about *The Way of the Heart* they go beyond this division. They go beyond a simplistic *either/or* division to place the mind inside the heart. Non-dual thinking doesn't reject the rational mind, it transcends and includes it. First-half of life teaching likes to proclaim ideals; second-half of life teaching meets people where they are. The ideals are not rejected, but they are interpreted with mercy and forgiveness. This is the wisdom of good pastoral practice and awareness. Not everyone is able to do this as we know from sad experiences in the Church today. The Franciscan, Richard Rohr, often points out that whenever God forgives us he is breaking his own rules!

The unique aspect of centering prayer is that it connects this re-wiring of the brain with the act of letting go. The evidence from the HeartMath Institute is that when the defensive attitude of the egoic operating system kicks in it creates a holding on, grasping and defensive attitude. Linked with what is called the reptilian brain, this is rooted in the need for survival. We then fall into the stance of defence or attack. This cuts us off from the highest intelligence and wisdom that we have as human beings. The opposite occurs when we can connect in a more relaxed way with the neural pathway that leads to the heart. Instead of clinging on, we open ourselves and yield to what is happening. To use more pious language we connect in the centre of our being with what we Christians call the Holy Spirit. So the basic stance is not closed, but open to what is happening, and that is precisely what happens over a period of time and practice with centering prayer. We don't cling to anything; we just let it go by returning to our sacred word. So the conclusion that Cynthia Bourgeault comes to is that this is not just for the mystics; it is a skill that belongs to a mature person.

This is what spiritual teachers claim today to be the missing path in Christianity. We quickly forget Jesus modelled for us – as we saw in the last chapter – and Christianity became largely another dualistic religion. We forget that it is the mind of Christ which we have been created to adopt and use as our way of seeing everything:

> Let the same mind be in you that was in Christ Jesus, who, though he was in the form of God did not regard equality with God as something to be exploited, but emptied himself being in the form of a slave being born in human likeness.[31]

He emptied himself, says Paul, which means that his basic stance before life was not a defensive clinging but a letting go. This kind of stance invites us to stop clinging to our self-righteousness, our own opinions, our grievances, especially the legitimate ones, which is so difficult for the *false-self.* It opens to the spirituality of complete self-giving in love for others, that was so characteristic of Jesus and what both Don Bosco and Mary Mazzarello sought to imitate and pass on to us.

Balancing Action and Contemplation

A contemplative spirituality doesn't ignore the mind; it desires to use it at its highest level in union with the heart. At its best, it demonstrates how mature religion can hold together both reason and loving-kindness in a very creative tension. It doesn't reject reason but places it inside the loving-kindness of the heart and unites the two. This is exactly how both Don

31 Ph 2: 5-7

Bosco and Mary Mazzarello lived their lives. Their evident holiness answered a question that can be legitimately asked of all those who seek to explore inner experience. It is the question of discernment, *How can I know that my inner experience is putting me in touch with the Holy Spirit or is it just an illusion?* It is a vital question. History is full of people claiming to hear the voice of God, yet living very delusional lives.

The answer comes from Jesus himself when he says *by their fruits you shall know them.* If our lives exhibit anxiety, fear, rigidity, and elitist behaviour, then we can be pretty clear this is not coming from God. If, on the other hand, our lives demonstrate love, joy, peace, patience, kindness and wisdom then we can be sure this is action of the Holy Spirit. Both Don Bosco and Mary Mazzarello provide clear evidence that their activities were steeped in the love of God; hence the joy and peace they radiated constantly in their lives. Those who lived with and knew Don Bosco remarked on his calm and peaceful demeanour. It was often said about him that when he was facing the most worrying troubles he appeared to be even more at peace. The same was true of Mary Mazzarello; she radiated serenity and joy. Both Sisters and the young felt uplifted in her presence. Both these Salesian founders gave the impression of being grounded in their *true-selves* where nothing could really touch them. Despite their many problems and difficulties they were both examples of what Paul describes as the *centred balanced life*:

> For I am convinced that neither death nor life, nor angels nor rulers, nor things present, nor things to come, nor powers, nor height, nor depth, nor anything else in all creation, will be able to separate us from the love of God in Christ Jesus our Lord.[32]

I know in my own experience when I am not truly centred and grounded in God then I get anxious and irritable. The *Martha* in me takes over and I get irritated and critical of others. This problem arises from a of lack of balance in my life when I give myself over to action and neglect my inner life. Action and contemplation should not be seen as opposites. They are two aspects of a balanced spirituality. Authentic inner experience

32 Romans 8:38-39

in prayer can never take us away from sharing in the pain and suffering in our world; in fact, the opposite is true. As we see with Don Bosco and Mary Mazzarello the more we care for others, the more God cares for us. Instead of lying dormant the gifts of the Holy Spirit come alive in our souls and our hearts and minds are transformed into a new way of seeing God's presence in all people and in all things.

Mature religion should move us to a place of compassionate seeing where I can confront my own demons, self-centredness, self-righteousness, my own point of view, and learn to forgive the dark side of who I am in the safe knowledge that I am Beloved of God and loved unconditionally at all times. When I am not afraid to go down into the deepest part of my soul I too will encounter my own wild beasts and woundedness, but I will also be led to experience the angels of God's compassionate love ministering to me. I am ready for mission. But I need to keep going back to make the connection between prayer and action as Jesus did throughout his ministry.

Chapter 6 – A Relational God

> The community is a reflection of the mystery of the Trinity: there we find a response to the deep aspirations of the heart, and we become for the young signs of love and unity.[33]
>
> Our community of Daughters of Mary Help of Christians – a specific expression of the ecclesial community – finds the deepest reason for its existence in the mystery of the Blessed Trinity. It lives the spirituality of the Preventive System creating a family atmosphere.[34]

One of the most exciting developments in contemporary spirituality and theology is a new interest in the mystery of the Trinity, and a recognition that it is foundational to everything, not just to the spiritual journey, but to everything that exists. In the last chapter I wrote about the need for a new way of seeing, and the need to move beyond the binary systems and the narrow perspective of the egoic operating system with its emphasis on differences, on what is inner and outer, them and me, right and wrong. We are born with this kind of brain, but we do have within us the capacity to upgrade to a different way of seeing which is the way of the heart, or the eye of the heart as some call it. This is not about feelings but recognising that the heart is an organ of perception. Used in this way it aligns us with the deepest reality of things which, as the quantum scientists are increasingly telling us, is that everything is connected. In handing on to us the Salesian family spirit, Don Bosco was in tune with this way of living.

This alignment is strongly reflected in the Constitutions of both the Salesians and the Salesian Sisters in terms of community life. The SDB article connects the mystery of the Trinity with the deep aspirations of the heart and how this finds expression in our love for the young. The FMA article teaches that the deepest reason for human existence is to share in the mystery of the Trinity. Together with the SDB Constitutions the article goes on to say that this deep identification with the mystery of

33 Article 49 SDB Constitutions

34 Article 36 FMA Constitutions

God flows out naturally into our apostolic work. Here we find a Salesian spirituality that makes a strong connection between union with God and action on behalf of the young. This union of action and contemplation is, I believe, at the heart of a renewed understanding of the Preventive System which has the twofold aim of educating the young in the faith and at the same time pointing the way towards a second-half of life spirituality, at the heart of which is a shift in understanding from a moral understanding of religion to a mystical one.

In this chapter I want to reflect more deeply on the mystery of the Trinity. The great twentieth century theologian, Karl Rahner, famously said that *if the Pope were to inform us Catholics that we no longer had to believe in the mystery of the Trinity it would have no practical implication for the way we live our lives.* If this is true, and I think it is, then it is sad because it means we are missing so much. It also may explain why we sometimes turn our Salesian spirituality into a charter for workaholics. Reflection on the Trinity helps us to restore a better balance to our busy active lives. This mystery is the central pattern and shape of how we relate to God and it should have profound practical implications for the way we relate to God, the way we relate to others, and the way we relate to the whole of creation.

The Trinity will always be a mystery way beyond our understanding but at the same time there is a fascination in all of us that seeks connection with this mystery. Philosophers and theologians tell us that *like always attracts like.* Our faith tells us that we have all been created in the image and likeness of God. Our deepest DNA is from God. The mystics and saints have long known this. *I thank you for the wonder of my being* sang the psalmist. Augustine spoke of God as *closer to me than I am to myself.* The author of the Cloud of Unknowing declares with amazing frankness *God is your being and what you are, you are in God.* For John of the Cross the soul's centre is God. Yahweh tells Jeremiah, *Before I formed you in the womb I knew you.* And Jesus himself lives from this deep union with his Father which he extends also to us, *On that day you will know that I am in my Father and you in me and I in you.*

We have all been taught that mystery is something that is not knowable. In fact mystery is something that is infinitely knowable. We can never say that we have it all worked out in our heads, but we can deepen our understanding as we discover that this foundational mystery always invites our participation. What we are finding today is that many of our scientists are confirming what the mystics have always known. As they examine the structure of reality and speak to us about atoms and molecules, protons and neutrons, what is fascinating seems to be the space between them as they move in relationship. Reality at its most basic level is relational. We live in a profoundly relational world, and the same seems to be the case for the unfolding mysteries of the universe with its billions of galaxies, black holes, planets and stars. The more we discover about the universe, the less we seem to know. We are led into endless mystery, tremendous and awesome, and yet deeply intimate as we discover that we too are stardust. We are just a small, tiny, but conscious part of this wonderful mystery of creation.

We are learning a new humility after a long and distracting time in our history when we have proclaimed our autonomy and individuality. In our Church teaching and catechesis we have been led to believe that we are separate from God and the whole point of religion then becomes an individual struggle to get back to this distant God by performing our religious duties well. We had to find the right doctrines to believe, to practise correct behaviour and morality, and perform the right rituals. This emphasis on what we had to do has led us, I believe, into the current imbalance in our spiritual lives where work has not just weakened our prayer life but reduced it in large measure to a means of getting God to do what we want. Our reliance on doing, even in prayer, meant that prayer has basically been reduced to saying prayers.

The view from the saints and the mystics is very different. We are not separate from God. We are all deeply united. The whole sweep of mature religion is to help us to realise this more consciously. Jesus is the second member of the Holy Mystery that we call God and as the image of the Father he takes on human form to tell us that we are all beloved sons and beloved daughters. Jesus puts it all together, the human and the divine, the material and the spiritual and invites us to follow him. That is surely what the theological word *salvation* means. Once we grasp this – which is what we really mean by faith – it introduces us to a whole new way of seeing and living. We are no longer living and struggling within the limited horizon of our individual lives, we move to an awareness of the great spaciousness that is the mystery of God constantly flowing forth from God as Father into the Son and into the Spirit and into us. Jesus becomes the connection point that plugs us into the amazing mystery of the give-and-take of love that we call God.

It is interesting to note that it took the Church the best part of three hundred years before it could formally and theologically articulate a Trinitarian formula of belief. One of the first words used by the Fathers of the Church was the Greek word *perichoresis* which means dance, a wonderfully attractive word to describe the flow and interaction of everything. Western thought, however, was much more influenced by Aristotle who described the human being primarily as a *substance*. He also added the relational dimension but with *substance* implying individuality and independence you can see which one won the argument. The relational element lost influence and with serious consequences as we still experience today in our spirituality of the body and sexuality. I will examine this more in a later chapter.

When Constantine established Christian pre-eminence in Europe in the fourth century the Church increasingly adopted the monarchical view of the Trinity with God the Father at the top of the triangle, and the authority structures of the Church followed the same hierarchical pattern. I can't help wondering how Jesus would react to titles such as *Your Eminence, Your Grace, My Lord* and so on. It seems a long way from Paul's brilliant description of Jesus' path as one of self-emptying love – *kenosis*. Clearly I am not suggesting that members of the hierarchy do not live self-sacrificing lives, but in today's democratic world it does seem to get in the way of the message. Today the medium is very much the message.

As this was happening in the Western Church, one group that did seem to get the path followed by Jesus was the contemplative wisdom school of the East in Cappadocia, whose leading lights included Basil of Caesarea, Gregory of Nyssa, and Gregory of Nazianzus. Their teaching didn't start by looking at the individual persons of the Trinity but at the flow of energy between the persons, in other words at the relationships. They saw the Trinity as an endless flow of self-emptying love, and this is the *perichoresis* at the heart of the holy mystery that we call God. It emphasises movement, mutuality, intimacy, communion.

Our Western understanding lacked much of this intimate, relational language. Our theology was more speculative and abstract, hence the divorce from the everyday spirituality of ordinary people which largely forgot the Father and the Spirit and focussed exclusively on Jesus as God. Today we are recovering a better understanding of this mystery. As well as pointing to the relational dimension in God we can say that God IS relationship. This has rich implications for how we balance our lives in our Salesian spirituality.

We are not just individuals, or even teams of people, for that matter, busily working away for God like an army of ants. Salesian spirituality is not a dutiful performance in which we rack up our good deeds to keep us on the right side of God's acceptance. We are a constant part of the flow of life and love that pours out and is being constantly given back by Father, Son and Spirit. This flow of love is happening in every single person on the planet. Many are not consciously aware of this, and this can be true of many baptised persons. This does not make them bad people but it deprives them of the immense joy of consciously drawing on this flow of life within.

In many retreat houses and religious houses you often find a copy of Rublev's icon of the Trinity with its three figures gazing with respect and love across a table eating from a common bowl. On closer inspection you can see what art historians have identified as a small space on the front of the table to which there was once glued a mirror. The meaning seems clear: there was room at the table for a fourth, for humanity, that reflects God's presence and image. We don't just look at the dance of life from the side-lines; we are invited to join in the movement and dance, through Jesus our brother. This dance also includes the whole of creation so there is no splitting off, no separation between us, creation and God. We are learning that everything came forth from this divine dance and everything is taken back into it. We are all a bit fascinated by the work taking place at Cern in Switzerland in which an international group of scientists have built a giant Hadron Collider to try to discover the missing particle that helped matter to evolve after the Big Bang. Some have even called it the *God particle.* We Christians already have our God particle: it is the energy of love from which everything has evolved and which sustains everything in being.

There can be only one truth and what we are discovering today is that this pattern of connection, flow and relationship is revealed in everything that exists. The doctrine of the Trinity which appeared in the past as a bit distant and remote is now discovered in everything that we are experiencing, both in the smallest atoms and in the largest galaxies, in the sun and in the moon, in the beat of our hearts and the flow of our blood. The foundational nature of all reality is relationship. As the Eastern Fathers said, *Start with the relationship.* That is where the energy lies, and that is just what the quantum scientists seem to be confirming.

Community Life

There is certainly plenty of material about Salesian community life. It was the specific theme of the 25th General Chapter for the Salesians, but as the Rector Major wisely pointed out we cannot really change our communities by producing documents, and we have certainly produced plenty of documents. In the light of the growing reflection on the Trinity, I think it can be helpful to focus on the relational dimension of community life. It cautions us about the dangers of our Salesian activism, the *heresy* identified by Fr Chávez. Excessive work will always weaken community life and prevent it from being the transformative force for a spirituality such as ours that calls itself relational. If the Constitutions of the Salesian family place community life firmly in the orbit of the Trinity, we need to take on board everything that flows from this. In the next chapter I will reflect on the *active/contemplative* balance in our lives. For now I would suggest that a contemplative practice can really assist our Salesian community life.

Communities will always be a place where the ideal meets the real. We know that our apostolic work as Salesians is the place where we meet God in the young and the poor. We Salesians and Salesian Sisters, are called by our Constitutions to live this commitment in and through community life. We are told that God calls us into community and it is meant to be a place of joy and happiness. In reality, however, this may not always be the case. In our work with the young we are usually in the dominant position as adults. Ideally we try also to listen and learn from the young and the poor, but inevitably the flow is more often from us to them, as we try to guide them through the issues of the first-half of life. Here we are operating as fathers, brothers, or sisters, and the role is influential and tends to shape how we identify ourselves.

In community, the dynamic is very different. We are with fellow adults and we cannot hide our identity in our roles. We appear as we are and the community is the place where our shadow is revealed. It is a place of vulnerability. When people speak of the wonderful Father A or the incredible Sister B those who live with them might take a different view. *Try living with them!* This should not alarm us too much. We all have our shadow sides and if we can own them and acknowledge them it enables us to mature in the spiritual life. There is no real spiritual growth without this self-critical thinking. As we saw in an earlier chapter, the Salesian Preventive System is not just a method of working with the young it is a spirituality that if lived authentically takes us into to the second-half of life. The danger with activism is that we can use it to hide from this growth in consciousness: our work hides our vulnerability.

I am convinced that a spiritual practice of contemplative prayer is a crucial tool in moving us from the first-half of life to the second. As we move from morality to mysticism we discover our identity not so much in our working roles but at the much more foundational level of who we are in God. We tend to spend a lot of time asking the *what* question. What do I have to do to prove I am a good follower of Don Bosco or Mary Mazzarello, what is my role, what do I have to do? If we look at the lives of these two saints we find them less concerned about what they were doing but *who* was doing it with them. Because of their deep union with God they were fully conscious of who they were in God. Their apostolic work flowed out of this deep union. Consequently they were both at pains to create an authentic family-spirit that excluded no one, because all shared in a common identity as sons and daughters of God.

Mary was very concerned to stamp out any hierarchical ambitions, all those comparisons that the dualistic mind slips into. She declared that Salesian Sisters are:

> neither Madames nor Mademoiselles, nor poor things nor poor little ones! We are all sisters of the same family, daughters of the same Father and equally consecrated to Jesus Christ. And we must all work equally, love each other and be prompt to sacrifice ourselves.[35]

This sense of sisterly equality before God prompted Mary to warn against knee-jerk critical judgements of others. A Trinitarian community is one in which each person's differing talents and gifts are recognised but all are rooted in the same body of Christ. If corrections are to be made they are made out of loving-kindness, not anger, still less contempt. Mary Mazzarello was fully aware of her own frailty and shadow side and, even as the Superior, if she was at fault she would humbly apologise before other Sisters.

In similar vein we could allude to many positive and encouraging pieces of advice that Don Bosco gave about community life, but in view of our current situation in the Western World, it is useful to remind ourselves of some remarks Don Bosco made to the second General Chapter in 1880 about the reality of Salesian community life. They could have been written today.

> Vocations have been declining at a frightening rate, throughout the Church at large and unfortunately among us. There was a time when, if a young man showed the least sign of a vocation on coming to us, we were able in most instances to bring him

35 Carlo Colli *The Spirit of Mornese* (Don Bosco Publications New Rochelle NY 1982) p92

> along, mould him according to our spirit, and make him a priest. This is no longer the case. There is evidence, stronger by the day, that our schools, little by little, are going the way of all other schools. Our pupils today are no longer driven by that impulse towards good, towards religious practice, and towards imitating their religious educators, which was so much in evidence in olden times. How are we, then, to reverse this trend, so that vocations can be fostered as before?[36]

The answer Don Bosco goes on to give to his own question is not that Salesians must work harder. It is to renew our spirit of community, a reminder that we must treat each other and all confreres with mutual charity and gentleness, and let that community experience of forgiving and accepting love flow out into our ministry. Today we would describe this advice as placing us firmly back inside a Trinitarian spirituality. The Holy Mystery that we call God is a mystery of participation. We don't initiate this flow, we receive it before we can pass it on to others.

We have tended to address God as *Almighty* in many of our prayers but there is an incredibly challenging remark made by St Paul in his first letter to the Corinthians:

> God's foolishness is wiser than human wisdom, and God's weakness is stronger than human strength.[37]

What is Paul talking about here? God's foolishness, God's weakness? This kind of language is coming straight out of second-half of life transformation. As human beings we naturally admire strength and self-sufficiency. Both men and women today want to be autonomous, to be independent. We rarely hear preachers speaking about the weakness of God. I can't recall hearing homilies or talks about it. But theologians today are describing God's weakness as *inter-being*. Human strength admires holding on, and that may be necessary at times, but the mystery of the Trinity is more concerned with letting go, which does indeed look like weakness. Where we like autonomy, the mystery of the Trinity reveals mutual dependence. We like to achieve control over our lives, the

36 Ian Murdoch *Starting Again from Don Bosco* (Don Bosco Publications, UK 2009) p61
37 1 Cor 1:25

Trinity seems to prefer vulnerability.

I don't think we can do this unless we make a better connection between our inner lives and our outer lives, between our work and our prayer. When we do this it takes away our need to identify with our roles, for recognition, for praise for what we do, and teaches us that our identity is received rather than achieved. The language Jesus uses is purely relational, Father, Son, and Spirit. I can only be a son or a daughter in relationship with another, with the Father. When we are caught up in our work – however apostolic it may be – we tend to become possessive: *This is my mission; I will run it my way.* With God we get total disclosure and mutuality. We like to put boundaries around our own territory, God seems to push beyond all boundaries when one is three and three are one, and we cannot get our rational heads around that.

The need to find a new balance in our lives between action and contemplation is a pressing need today and we will examine this in our next chapter.

Chapter 7 – Active and Contemplative

> The third millennium: a time for mystics! It will be the depth of men and women moved by the Spirit that will save the meaning of life and challenge the limitations of our human vision.[38]

These are not days for business as usual; we are living through liminal times – times of profound change. Liminal times are threshold times when we stand between two rooms, with a foot in both. They are times of great uncertainty. Many of our trusted institutions seem unable to cope or chart a way forward. The task of mature religion is to help us to find meaning in new situations, to provide reasons for hope especially for the younger generations. This should be a central Salesian task. We need people who can move into the second-half of life and help others to do the same. Religious institutions are being challenged to take on a more prophetic role and in Fr Vecchi's words, help us to uncover the true meaning of life today and challenge the limitations of our human vision. For this to happen, I think that we need to move from morality to mysticism and to do this we need a better balance between action and contemplation.

If you examine classic spiritual stories the pattern is always the same. The hero passes through several stages which today are called levels of consciousness. He begins with simple consciousness, then is challenged to move into more complex consciousness, and finally he reaches enlightened consciousness, which looks similar to the first level but in fact is very different. My argument in this book is that this same pattern can be found in our Salesian Preventive System and understood in this sense it provides a way to respond to the challenge laid down by Fr Vecchi and Fr Chávez to integrate contemplation into our active spirituality and find a new way of seeing.

In the first-half of life reason, law and tradition hold sway, but it is a rather naïve simplicity. Things tend to be black-and-

38 Fr Juan Vecchi *Acts of the General Council* (Jan-March 2001) p19

white, there is little room for complexity. Contradictions and paradoxes haven't yet challenged our world view. Our vision, as Fr Vecchi says, is necessarily limited. The middle years will inevitably lead us into these paradoxes as we struggle with love, sin, failure, imperfection, mystery and deeper questions start to emerge. Mature religion should teach us at this point that the great spiritual task is not the slaying of other people's dragons, but learning to live with and embrace our own. This is what the prophets taught and it made them very unpopular; and it was the same with Jesus. We cannot achieve spiritual success by our own efforts, by willpower alone. We can't really change anybody else; we are asked to change ourselves. Nor can we change ourselves in terms of the limited vision of the *false-self.* If we can negotiate this part of the journey properly, we learn that the mystery of transformation does not work in spite of our woundedness, it works in it and through it. To succeed, we have to fail, and our ego hates failure. In the classic stories of searching, the hero never reaches enlightenment by doing courses of study. It is only when he sustains some wounds and experiences some disappointments.

This is counter-intuitive to our twenty-first century rational minds. We don't want to look at our flawed selves, so the classic avoidance pattern is to plunge into our work. Work is not bad, in fact it is good and necessary, and both Don Bosco and Mary Mazzarello set an amazing example of apostolic work on behalf of the young. Work itself is not the problem. So what is the problem? It all comes down to a question of balance, of integration. I have already alluded to the fact that both these saints lived lives of deep union with God, and it is clear that they both exhorted their followers to balance action and contemplation. Without this balance, our egos will remain in control and the danger of excessive work is that it reinforces our hunger for success and acclaim.

This is the classic *false-self* agenda, and if the *false-self* is difficult for us to acknowledge, the religious *false-self* is even more difficult to bring into the open, because the religious *false-self* loves to fit God into its own agenda. It is as the serpent told Adam and Eve, *You can be like God,* or Peter on Mount Tabor saying, *This is great, Lord, let's stay here.*

The religious *false-self* can even use the inner experience of prayer to keep us from the transformation that can only really come from engaging with reality, with life, with suffering, with failure, what Jesus calls *going to Jerusalem*. There is nothing more dangerous than a *false-self* claiming God on its side. The pharisees do it throughout the Gospel; the religious fanatics of today and throughout history justify violence in this way. What makes the teaching of the prophets so radical and so crucial is that they tell us that we all do this in one way or another in our spiritual lives. A life of activism, yes, even Salesian activism, can easily domesticate the transformational message of the Gospel into my own agenda. At the same time a life of Salesian contemplation without any active ministry of sharing and living with others can equally put God into my own little box of *spirituality*. It is always a question of balance between the inner and outer life.

The prophets railed against any form of idolatry that placed another god before Yahweh. In our sophisticated times we may think we have outgrown idolatry but perhaps a more accurate word to describe our situation is *addiction*. Anne Wilson Schaef said many years ago that not only do we all suffer from some form of addiction but the same is true of the society we live in. Richard Rohr[39] has linked this notion of addiction with the biblical understanding of the word *sin*. He suggests that rather than see sin as something God has to punish, it is more like a disease or a sickness. Jesus himself uses this kind of language when he says that he hasn't come for the healthy but for the sick.

Christians focus a lot of attention more on the teachings of Jesus in the Gospels. We often forget that so much of his ministry was about healing. When I taught religious education in our Salesian High School in Bootle, Merseyside, I used to teach a course on marriage to the older students. I would show a videotape of a couple who had only been married a short time, but whose relationship seemed to be deteriorating. The husband was a farmer and he spent all his time working out in the fields. When he came home at night he was too exhausted to talk to his wife. He was obviously working too hard, but

39 Richard Rohr *Breathing under Water* (St Anthony Messenger Press Ohio 2011)

what was interesting was his complete lack of awareness of his neglect of his wife. In fact he felt that all his work was geared to supporting the marriage. He hadn't realised that all relationships require real communication if they are not to stagnate.

The problem with an activist spirituality is that it can all too easily use work, even apostolic work, as a way of avoiding the problem of addiction. Addiction is not just about drugs or alcohol abuse but more importantly it lays bare the essential pain of the human condition which can never be avoided. It lies in a deep-seated sense of unworthiness and shame, and can be found even in the people who appear superficially confident. This is what Jesus comes to heal in us. The very word *salvation* comes from *salus* meaning health. Some fundamentalist Christians present the idea of *being saved* as a great one-off experience. I think it is much more a gradual awakening to the amazing fact that God loves us unconditionally. That means that we are accepted at the deepest core of our being. No amount of work can achieve this; it is pure gift, it is grace. Once we accept this wonderful gift, this amazing grace as the hymn says, then our work flows from a different place and has a different quality. It is graced work.

Perhaps the most difficult addiction we all share is to our own thinking, our own point of view. We presume that our own way of thinking is correct, perfectly logical and reasonable. *Why can't others see this? Why don't others see reality the way we see it?* This form of addiction is so deep that it can truly be called *demonic* which might be a shock to us when we first realise it. On so many pages in the Gospel we find Jesus casting out devils. There are four references alone to demons in the first chapter of Mark's Gospel. If we are preachers of the Gospel we probably pass over these references as not really having anything to say to our sophisticated, rational times. But if we can see the repetitive nature of our behaviour and compulsive reactions to both people and situations we may see why Jesus is engaged in trying to free so many people from this kind of restriction to hearing and understanding his non-dual teaching and opening us to a new way of seeing.

The irony of ego consciousness is that it is not really consciousness at all, because it eliminates the unconscious. It wants to know and be certain and is not open to any kind of unknowing which all the mystics identify as the way into God. Our culture promotes intelligent and smart people who are often completely unaware of their unconscious motivations. The Church too promotes clever people who may not demonstrate much wisdom or compassion. True leaders are formed by the necessary falling and failure which leads to second-half of life wisdom. We have the classic example of Peter who seems to fail many times in the Gospels, and when he is finally *interviewed* by Jesus for the task of leading his followers, the questions are not about cleverness or intelligence, but love. And the question is repeated three times for emphasis. Great theologians such as Thomas Aquinas and John of the Cross remind us of this when they said that we cannot know God with our minds but only with love. The young French girl, Therese of Lisieux, became a Doctor of the Church by promoting her way in which she replaced performance related religion, by the spirituality of imperfection, what she called her *Little Way*. This is the change of mind-set that Jesus calls for, from ego consciousness to knowing with the heart.

The Contemplative Path

The recovery of the contemplative tradition that we are witnessing today in our world is a real sign of the Spirit awakening our hearts, our Church, and our culture to this new kind of consciousness. We are living in times of great technical sophistication which almost every day rolls out a new hi-tech gizmo to make our lives easier. It might seem strange that I am promoting contemplation in such an environment. People today are almost wedded to their smartphones, iPads and MP3 players as they seek connection through social network sites, text messaging and so on. None of these things are bad in themselves but they tend to keep us on the surface level of external stimulation. Recently, when going into a prison to celebrate Mass, the chaplain advised me not to give a long homily. Instead of preaching, he often lets the prisoners enjoy a few moments of silence, since it is the only silence they are ever allowed to enjoy inside prison. I couldn't help wondering if with all our freedom we get much experience of silence in our lives. The mystics call it the language of God. We seem to have lost this wisdom that can live with ambiguity and mystery and hold the necessary tension.

In his teaching on prayer Jesus clearly invites us into the experience of silence.

> Whenever you pray go into your room and shut the door and pray to your Father who is in secret; and your Father who sees in secret will reward you.[40]

He goes on to warn us not to get caught up in words; we are not to *babble like the pagans do.* So Jesus is not speaking about petitionary prayers, liturgical prayers or devotional prayers, good though they are. He wants to move us to a deeper level of awareness. He is leading beyond the *cataphatic* way of praying with words and images, to prayer beyond words and images, what became known as the *apophatic* tradition. In telling us that the Father is already there waiting for us he is revealing the most wonderful reality of the spiritual life: the divine indwelling. The gift is already given and Jesus is telling that there is nothing to be achieved, it is only to be enjoyed. True spirituality is not about the fruitless struggle for moral perfection. It is all about union now, which is tasted in prayer. The great discovery is that what we are seeking has already been found, hidden in the depths of our souls.

Our unworthiness, our moral imperfection, our vague sense of shame, of not coming up to the mark is not a problem for Jesus who clearly found God not in order and perfection but in disorder and imperfection and told us to do the same. The gift that is prayer is the medicine, the software, the reality, the cloud of unknowing, whatever image you want to use to describe an experience beyond words. In the very depths of our being God is healing, forgiving and transforming us. This is the place where we learn our true identity, our *true-self* which is always in union with God. In the depths of our heart and soul we learn that God desires a relationship of pure love.

---

40 Mt 6:6

It is important not to set impossible goals in our prayer with regard to time. For active busy Christians, spiritual teachers recommend twenty minutes a day. If you can't manage twenty do fifteen or even ten. But it should become a regular daily practice. The technique of contemplative prayer is very simple. We are invited to sit still, to quieten the mind and the body, to breathe slowly and naturally. When thoughts or emotions arise simply observe them and gently let them go, returning your loving attention to God with the aid of your sacred word. It doesn't matter how many distracting thoughts or emotions arise. Just observe them arising and falling. The key action is *kenosis*, the simple letting go of all thoughts and emotions. The act of *kenosis* places us in perfect alignment with the spirituality of the Jesus path, not clinging to anything.

Of course the ego will fight this. When a busy person sits still, the ego will flood the mind with thoughts, about all the things that have to be done; or with emotions such as anger, jealousy, even lustful thoughts that will invade the mind. Centering prayer has a particular contribution to make in the face of this problem. The technique is not to fight the thoughts because that only feeds the egoic mind even more, but to gently let them go. Here is where we Salesians can imitate in a most profound way the gentleness of our patron, St Francis of Sales.

It appears from the life of Mary Mazzarello that she prayed in this way. Sister Vergnaud, commenting on her union with God towards the end of her life, recalls this incident:

> I remember one day at recreation, we were gathered around her speaking of the poverty of the unforgettable house of Mornese, when a sister took the liberty of asking her: *Mother, what do you do in church with the thought of the house, and the needs and problems which seem ever on the increase?* She answered with all simplicity, *What do I do? By the grace of God those thoughts don't bother me in church!*[41]

Clearly Mary had found a way of dealing with distracting thoughts, however important or pressing they may have been.

Another trap which the egoic mind sets up is to get you to

41 *Cronistoria* edited by Sr Giselda Capetti FMA, (Don Bosco Publications NY 1981) p266

evaluate your prayer time. Did I pray well or did I pray badly? It is important never to do this. You may have had one distracting thought after another. That is not the point. We never initiate prayer; in prayer, we awaken to and participate in the mutual prayer and love that is the life of the Trinity. When we are sitting in silent prayer, God is at work healing our unconscious. If this kind of prayer is practised on a daily basis there can be no doubt that the gifts of the Spirit will come alive and the mind of Christ, as Paul calls it, awakens in us. There is a clear shift from the narrow point of view of the calculating self-centred *false-self,* to the Great Spaciousness, the Great Compassion, the Great Mercy, the Great Wisdom, the great Love that is God. We begin to experience, however fleetingly, our *true-self.* The *false-self* will not go away, but the *true-self* can absorb it and we become more conscious, more aware of when our *false-self* is dictating our reaction. The great and sure test that the image of God is working in us is when we meet someone whom we don't like and we can see the image of God in that person.

The problem with just using words in prayer is that it often reduces prayer to a mechanism for getting God to do things for us. In a sense, we are trying to get God to change. All prayer is good, but at its deepest level it is not about changing God but being willing to let God change us. It is about emptying the mind and opening the heart to whatever God wishes to do with us. It is becoming open and available to transformation.

Some might object that time in prayer takes us away from the many needs of the apostolate. In fact the opposite is true. If silent, contemplative prayer is in any way authentic it takes us into a deep intimacy with our relational God. The more we taste this experience the more we want to share life and love with others. When we experience the pure Being that is God, we learn to trust and recognise the being of the other in all situations.

The Grace of Unity

When Fr Viganò was the Rector Major he often spoke and wrote about the need for us Salesians to find a proper balance between prayer and action in our lives, what he called the grace of unity. Fr Vecchi and Fr Chávez have made the same point. There is no doubt that ours is an active spirituality but it contains the danger that action always comes first, before prayer. What happens then is that the agenda of the *false-self* takes over in our lives. No one gives a better example of the need for balance than Jesus who frequently left the crowds and went up into the hills to pray.

The Constitutions of the Salesian Sisters contain a five-point profile of the FMA in the mind of Don Bosco. He lists some characteristic Salesian virtues such as charity, patience, cheerfulness, and mortification. He then places these virtues inside an important template in these words:

> These virtues must be well tested and deeply rooted in the Daughters of Mary Help of Christians, because their lives must harmonize the contemplative and the active life reproducing Martha and Mary.[42]

Here we have in Don Bosco's own words the key elements of contemplation and action that make up a balanced Salesian spirituality. It is not surprising, therefore, to find the same sentiments in the Constitutions of the Salesian Congregation in one of the chapters describing how we Salesians are called to live the grace of unity:

> Attentive to the presence of the Spirit and doing everything for God's love he becomes like **Don Bosco a contemplative in action.**[43] (Author's emphasis)

Every spirituality, like every human being, has a shadow side, and while we promote and celebrate our hard work on behalf of the young, we have to be aware that there is a constant battle. Michael Winstanley describes it well:

> For Salesians, there is, I think a danger of being too busy being Samaritans to listen to the word with silent attentiveness, to go to the mountain of prayer. Often our busyness is tinged with over-anxiety, inducing stress and tension. In some cases one can detect symptoms of workaholism, incipient or verging on the chronic. This can entail a blurring of perspective, a loss of true focus. When there are clashes of priorities it tends to be

42 Constitutions and Regulations of the Daughters of Mary, Help of Christians p21
43 Constitutions of the Society of St Francis of Sales (Rome 1984) Article 12

> prayer that is jettisoned. Without times of prayer in which we listen to God's love, our apostolic ventures can become jobs or careers rather than ministries. We run the risk of building our own kingdoms rather than that of Jesus.[44]

The challenge might seem a very difficult one and we usually say that we just haven't got the time to devote to prayer, especially contemplative prayer when nothing seems to be happening. But that is the point. Prayer is not a place for our rather compulsive doing mode. It is about creating the space to let God do whatever he wants in our hearts and souls. It is really about getting our egos out of the way so that God can reveal our true identity to us as a free gift of grace: that we are beloved of God and God delights in us. Why resist that?

44 Michael T Winstanley *Don Bosco's Gospel Way* (Don Bosco Publications, UK 2002) p68

Chapter 8 – Friendship and Sexuality

> True friendship is liberating for friends and is truly a gift from God. It enables each person to grow in his or her identity and become the person he or she is called to be.[45]

> I don't call you servants any more. I call you friends because I have made known to you everything that I have heard from my Father.[46]

The words of Jesus are astonishing. They take us right into the heart of the Trinity, into the very intimacy of God's life. Jesus holds nothing back. Everything he has received from the Father is shared with us. It reminds us that we have been created for union with God and the gift has already been given to us. The spiritual journey is not so much about what we find and discover; it is much more a case of being found. It is not so much about trying to cling on to God as being held. Nor is it a private search for salvation; it is a shared knowing. Communication becomes communion. We have been created to be friends of God. This is not something we have to achieve. It is something we awaken to and realise.

All religions teach that human beings lack awareness of who they really are. We are sleepwalkers and the whole point of our religious rituals is to wake us up to the holy mystery of who we are in God. In our Christian faith we have the added gift of Jesus assuring us of God's friendship, of his desire to share intimacy with us, of his unconditional love. He tells us that the Father will make his home in the deepest centre of our being. There he awaits us in secret.

Our human condition struggles to believe this amazing news. We feel that we are always separate from God, never quite worthy enough for friendship with God. We struggle to trust, which is really a failure of faith. Faith is not so much about doctrines and dogmas as trusting in the mystery of the reality and truth of God's love for us. The saints and the mystics are those who break through to this awareness as their daily

---

45 Eunan McDonnell *God Desires You* (Columba Press Dublin 2001) p117

46 Jn 15:16

reality. They reach a level of non-dualism that overcomes the sense of separation from God and enjoy the gift of union.

Many Christians struggle with the problem of dualism. We remain blocked in the first-half of life agenda by trying to root out our faults and work hard for God to prove our worthiness. This is holiness as willpower and it is doomed to fail. We listen to sermons, read books, make retreats and yet the sense of failure, of unease, of falling short remains. Religion becomes a home for a work ethic rather than a place of intimacy. It is all summed up in a sense of shame. If we work really hard perhaps God will accept us. I think that much of this sense of unworthiness is located especially in our bodies, in the area of sexuality.

This is a real tragedy for Christians in particular, because we are the only religion that proclaims and teaches that God became a human being. Someone once said that if the devil wanted to destroy Christianity he could do no better than attack us in our bodies. Certainly it appears that our Christian teaching on sexuality has been seriously damaged by the dualistic mind-set.

If it is true to say that we are living in liminal times, a profound time of transition, then the need for healthy authentic teaching on sexuality must be a part of what is being called in the Church *new evangelisation.* At present the Church is still carrying the wound of sexual abuse by clergy and religious. This has turned many people away from the Church in anger and sadness. We know that abuse is certainly not confined to priests and religious – most abuse occurs within families. But because the clergy are supposed to provide moral leadership, the shock and scandal is much greater. Abuse has caused deep distress and trauma to victims and at the same time it has weakened the Church's voice in the area of sexual teaching. We have to honestly admit that much of the programmes in seminaries and formation houses were overly negative in the area of sexuality, and this was often all that was being passed on to the laity in the pews.

As Salesians, we have to be concerned at how this negative view of sexuality is damaging for young people as well as for ourselves since our spirituality is essentially relational. I have stressed in this book the importance of a *both/and* rather than *either/or* attitude to spirituality. Healthy formation in sexuality is a primary component of first-half of life spirituality. As we grow in years our sexual maturity ought to be growing with us. In the second-half of life it should flower into the beautiful gift of friendship and love that God has created us to enjoy. Sadly, today many young people are not listening to much of what the Church is teaching in this area. It was often remarked that while huge crowds of young people greeted John Paul II at World Youth Days with great enthusiasm, a significant number were not following what the Church was teaching in the area of sexual morality. I recall taking a group of young people to a conference on the Church's sexual teaching in the presence of Cardinal Basil Hume. He didn't condemn or attack the young people's views, he listened, and then as he spoke at the end of the meeting he said he would much prefer to be sitting down with each person individually and have a conversation.

Far be it from me to know the answer to these problems, but I would like to offer some thoughts from my experience – limited as it is – coming up to fifty years as a Salesian.

Sexuality and Spirituality

I think we need to recover the power and beauty of the word *sexuality* and one of the ways to do this is to link it strongly with the word *spirituality*. Sexuality and spirituality should not be portrayed as enemies; they are two aspects of the same coin: the search for union. They are two ways of naming the same reality, one through materiality and the other through soul or spirit. The dualistic mind seeks to oppose them; the non-dual mind sees them as aiming for the same thing: the search for otherness, the movement beyond the self into the holy mystery of relationship and union.

Increasingly, today there is need to emphasise the distinction between sexuality and genital activity. Sexuality is much broader and richer than genital activity. If the young turn their back on the Church's sexual teaching they are left to the mercy of the *anything goes* morality of the secular world. In the Salesian community where I live I see our parish clergy constantly opening doors to young mothers, often unmarried, appearing with their children asking for baptism. Sadly by the time the babies are being baptised the parents are not together.

The first-half of life agenda is built on creating necessary boundaries, rules and guidance that help to put necessary safeguards round the powerful mystery that is human sexuality. Too many young people are left with the urge to have genital sex with little or no idea of the power and beauty of an enduring relationship of friendship with its inevitable highs and lows, its joys and sorrows, and its enormous potential for growth. My concern in this book is with adult Salesian spirituality and it seems to me that if we are to help our young people through the current situation we need to have matured sufficiently in our own sexuality, and particularly in the area of friendship and love.

Language and Love

One of our problems in the English language is that we only have one word for love. The Greek language gives us four words each with different nuances of meaning. The first word *eros* describes the erotic energy of love. Erotic energy has had a bad press in Christian spirituality denoting passion and desire, which were judged as dangerous. Erotic energy is not bad in itself, it always depends on the context. You can be actively engaged in genital sex with no real eroticism. This is to use sexuality as a means of dealing with human pain and loneliness. In the same way you can be full of erotic energy yet not involved in genital sex. *Eros* means life and energy. It is interesting to see that Pope Benedict XVI used the word positively in his beautiful encyclical, *God is Love.*[47]

Eros is an expression of life and vitality. You can see it in someone's eyes. Someone involved in trivial sex has little vitality in their eyes. To be active sexually with many partners is much easier and less challenging than to be involved in a committed relationship. In a true relationship of love you have to make space in yourself for another. You learn how to receive someone else's feelings. Many people today are so caught up

---

47 *Deus Caritas Est, God is Love*, Benedict XVI CTS

in their pain, they are unable to receive the pain of another.

Storge is a Greek word meaning liking. It usually refers to a liking for things. It is what is meant by the word *cute*. Some people go through life deciding what they like or don't like. It's not very deep and it won't get you far on the spiritual journey.

Philia is the word for friendship. It includes mutuality, support, understanding, joy, fun, sharing, acceptance and the laughter and tears that are part of all human relating as we share our joys and sorrows. I have often said on many retreats that while I was often warned about the danger of special friendships in my time of formation, I cannot recall ever being warned about the dangers of not having friends. There was wisdom of course in those warnings, but I recall giving a retreat in a Salesian province when a priest who had just celebrated his golden jubilee, wept openly in front of me because after fifty years of priesthood he had no friends. How sad.

We are fortunate in our Salesian spirituality to have the wonderful example of spiritual friendship given to us by St Francis of Sales. Francis seems to have reached a non-dual understanding of the gift of friendship. He did not regard genuine love for another as a hindrance to loving God. He taught that we don't have two hearts, one to love God and one to love our neighbour. Love is one, and divine and human love are intimately connected. Like the saints and mystics, Francis understood love as expanding the heart and inviting us into the mystery of participation that is the Trinity, and the give-and-take of love. This is the big mystery, the big pattern, that healthy religion leads us to. It is the second-half of life agenda when life can be lived out of love and not fear. Our capitalist society tells us that the world is one of scarcity; Jesus tells us that God's world is one of abundance. Love creates more love.

With Jane Frances de Chantal, Francis of Sales transformed a relationship of spiritual direction into a genuine friendship. They became what we today would call soul-friends. This is one of the greatest gifts that we can give to a world that is still obsessed with genital sexuality. This is why most people are called to marriage. There has to be an enduring quality to a loving relationship. In the early days, a romantic relationship is all sweetness and light, as we hide our less attractive side from the one we love, and they from us. Over time, this less attractive side is revealed and that is when real authentic love is born in forgiveness and mutual understanding. Here the prophetic side of the Preventive System comes alive: when the truth of who we are is revealed in and through our imperfections. If a couple can grow through these experiences of pain and hurt then love becomes truly healing and lovers really do become soul-friends.

What is encouraging today is that celibate religious are also discovering the wonderful gift of soul-friendship, both inside and beyond community. In reflecting on his friendship with Jane, Francis of Sales describes how their two spirits became one; both in their spiritual lives and in the founding of the Visitation Order. He describes this union of heart and spirit:

> This sacred fire which changes all into itself, wants to transform our hearts so that there be only love and we be no longer loving but love; no longer two but only one, since love unites all things in sovereign unity.[48]

Francis and Jane seem to have reached a beautiful integration of *eros* and *philia* in their love for God and for each other. Rather than get in the way of their love for others, their mutual love strengthened and sustained their love for others and shaped their holiness.

As we are moving beyond the more negative and restrictive understanding of spiritual friendship we are recognising the need that all of us have for this gift. Made in the image and likeness of our relational God, the ability to grow into a mature, supportive and enduring friendship is a key part of our understanding and experience of how God loves us. Francis of Sales gives that wisdom a welcome stamp of approval. Friendship is revelatory of how God loves us.

Agape is the fourth word the Greeks provide for the understanding of love. This kind of love takes us beyond the mutual give-and-take of friendship and moves us to a more challenging level of loving service. Christian spirituality has

---

48 Quoted in Eunan McDonnell *God Desires You* (Columba Press Dublin 2001) p122

seized on this word as an image of God's unconditional love. This kind of love moves beyond any personal agenda and the question of what's in it for me? This is the realm of self-giving, self-sacrificing love, and it is what clearly drove both Don Bosco and Mary Mazzarello in their commitment to the young and in all their apostolic labours.

In a real sense, *agape* could be used as a synonym for God. This is the love of *caritas* and the Christian tradition has consistently said that it is a gift. It cannot be earned and is experienced when we deal fully and openly with reality. This is always a mixture of joy and pain, and *agape* usually grows when we encounter some kind of sacrifice or suffering. It is what drives Salesians to care for the challenging poor, those who may not be very appealing, attractive or grateful. In fact they may even fight us and we may encounter them in our schools and other areas of ministry.

There may be times when we just don't know how to connect with some aggressive or angry young people. We might have tried all the relational love that we have but it doesn't seem to work. I think such moments are incredibly significant in the spiritual journey. We all like to be popular, to be successful, to be liked, but the danger is that it just bolsters the *false-self.* In such moments of bewilderment we cannot just work harder; what is needed is the help of a higher power.

Contemplative Prayer

To come through such trials we have to be people of prayer. Whatever kind of prayer gets you there is fine but in my experience this is where contemplative prayer takes us to a place where we are more open to the transforming power of God's love. Religious life has an inbuilt wisdom here, which we call the three vows, which are more or less a fixed pattern for all religious orders and congregations. Each vow has an internal and external dimension, but it is the inner life of the vows which is nourished by contemplative prayer.[49] Although Don Bosco preferred the order of obedience, poverty and chastity, and the FMA Constitutions use chastity, poverty and obedience, I like the rhythm of poverty, chastity and obedience.

49 Michael Cunningham *Within & Without* (Don Bosco Publications UK 2002) chapters 7-9

I think that poverty is the vow that empties us of the *false-self,* and prepares us to receive God's love through the vow of chastity, and finally this received love is shared with others through the vow of obedience in our mission and activity. Then the whole cycle continues as we have to go back into the letting go and emptying of poverty to receive even more love to share with others.

I place poverty at the beginning because unless we empty ourselves before God we are not really able to receive the love of *agape.* If our glass is full of our activities there isn't much room for God, and we may end up like the pharisee in the temple glorying in our good deeds. I see chastity as the connecting hinge that holds together our poverty and our obedience. It's all about love. We could be both very poor and very obedient b*ut without love,* as St Paul tells us, *we are nothing.* I also think that the experience of erotic desire and filial love give real shape and warmth to the love of *agape.* Of course, none of us can get this perfectly right all the time which is why the wheel of the vows keeps turning and deepening.

Sexuality and Wholeness

If we are to integrate our sexuality and our spirituality we need to overcome the dualisms of the past and seek wholeness. Aristotle's clear distinction between soul and body was taken up by influential Christian theologians such as Augustine who created an unhealthy split between body (bad) and spirit (good). Sexual sin was often understood in that sense. What had to be avoided at all costs were the *sins of the flesh,* but these sins of weakness didn't seem to worry Jesus too much as he associated with prostitutes and sinners. In fact, he seemed to have more difficulty with *sins of the spirit* such as intellectual pride, rigidity, hard-heartedness, and lack of forgiveness. You can meet some very religious people who are not very compassionate and forgiving.

Heresies such as Manichaeism and Jansenism have further widened the unhealthy split between body and spirit and the world has reacted to this by going to the opposite extreme of excessive sensuality. In Don Bosco's time Jansenism was still a baleful influence. In recovering the gift and beauty of friendship we can teach our young people that sexuality doesn't mean possessive love. We can recognise the beauty and attraction of the other without wanting to possess him or her.

Nor need we fear the erotic quality of authentic love. I'm always amused coming across a reading in the liturgy taken from the Song of Songs. The lectionary always provides an alternative reading! It seems that we are embarrassed by this unashamedly erotic book which the Jewish people placed in their scriptures – and we in ours. It is so encouraging to find Pope Benedict XVI referring to this book at the beginning of his encyclical letter *God is Love*. He strongly emphasises the need to heal the dualistic split of body and soul. Both need each other for authentic love. He warns both against embracing the body and rejecting the spirit, and equally against the false embrace of spirit that rejects the body. We are fully human, as persons that unite both body and spirit. He uses the Song of Songs to highlight the use of two Hebrew words to describe love in these love poems. One of these words is *dodim* suggesting a love that is insecure, needy and searching. The other word is *ahaba* which the Greek version of the Old Testament translates as *agape*.

This describes a growth of love from a rather needy, self-centred searching to the self-giving love of the other which seeks the love of the beloved. The Pope recognises that none of us can live by self-sacrificing love alone. We cannot always give, we must also receive. He uses the metaphor of Jacob's ladder: *eros* is an ascending love of desire; *agape* is a descending love that we receive from God and which we then share with others. He goes on to say that the more these two are unified the more authentic love is experienced.

Perhaps today we are recognising also that this holistic combination of *eros* and *agape* is even healthier when integrated with the love of friendship (*philia*). I am always struck by the different levels of friendship found in the life of Jesus. There is no doubt that Jesus demonstrates the highest form of *agape* love as he lays down his life for all. But the Gospels describe different circles of intimacy that he enjoyed. He shares some things with the fairly large group called disciples. He shares his most intimate teaching with the inner group called the apostles. The Gospels go on to describe an even more intimate friendship with one called the beloved disciple.

He also enjoys close friendship with the group of women that Luke says travelled with him and his disciples. He shares intimacy and friendship with Martha and Mary, with Mary of Bethany (possibly the same Mary), and with Mary Magdalene who is the first witness of the Resurrection and is rightly called the apostle to the apostles. He is totally at ease with the Samaritan woman and not afraid to speak with her on his own. Whenever he meets women he usually tells them to stand, to rise, to own their dignity as daughters of Abraham. When he meets men he often invites then to come down off their pedestals.

To know the Father of Jesus we must be capable of relationships. Sexuality and spirituality are both schools of relationship. To become fully human, we must be capable of creating space inside us for another; to be able to give and to receive. It is possible to be very religiously observant, but if we are not able to receive another at a deep level of soul it is doubtful how deeply we can receive our relational God. If I am so filled with my own agenda, my own opinions, my own ideas, my own reputation, how can I be sufficiently poor and empty to receive God? There is no intellectual technique or knowledge for this. We cannot use laws, asceticism, or commandments to avoid the scary world of relating to other human beings.

Because if I get close to you I will discover the terror and vulnerability of the human heart and I will know that I can't fix you and you can't fix me, and I may discover that the world is so complicated that I want to retreat to my world of work and activity. In calling us to faith, Jesus is asking us to trust in the holy mystery of a God whose very Being is given and received in total loving disclosure. God is a mystery of communion and the invitation to contemplation is an invitation to the cosmic dance that is going on all around us. If we can integrate *eros*, *philia*, and *agape*, we can even find room for a little bit of *storge* love as we decorate our homes, feed our pets and change the colour of the curtains!

Chapter 9 – Holiness and Failure

> Young people of every continent, do not be afraid to be the saints of the new millennium! Be contemplatives, love prayer; be coherent with your faith and generous in the service of your brothers and sisters, be active members of the Church and builders of peace.[50]

> The saints are the true reformers. Now I want to express this is an even more radical way; only from the saints, only from God does true revolution come, the definitive way to change the world.[51]

If young people are to respond to Pope John Paul's challenge to become contemplatives then someone has to teach them. If we are living and modelling an adult Salesian spirituality we have to give this serious consideration in our personal lives and our formation programmes. This is one of the central challenges of these liminal times in which we find ourselves. We often say that it is the young who will shape the future and if we really are educators and evangelisers of the young we have to offer them guidance and, even more importantly, the witness of our own lives. The challenges set out by both Pope John Paul II and Pope Benedict XVI to the youth of the world are therefore also addressed to us. This is authentic second-half of life teaching in which wisdom is passed on to future generations.

We are all aware of the vocation crisis in the Western World. Despite all our prayers and efforts little seems to change. Some congregations are just dying out. I have preached quite a few retreats to communities that have taken in sisters of a similar charism whose own orders seem to be in terminal decline. We see religious abandoning apostolates, and bishops closing or clustering parishes. So we redouble our prayers and efforts to get more vocations; after all, the work has to continue. Maybe this is missing something; perhaps the vocation crisis is saying

---

50 Pope John Paul II, *World Youth Day*, Rome 2000

51 Pope Benedict XVI, *World Youth Day*, Cologne 2005

something to us at a deep and profound level. Instead of asking for more bodies to do the work we could begin to ask ourselves what God might be saying to us through the vocation crisis. Perhaps God is asking us to live more integrated lives.

As we get older and struggle with failing energy and health we tend to think that our best Salesian years are behind us. We look back fondly at when we were in the thick of active ministry. But the common task of the second-half of life is to pass on wisdom to the next generation. Wisdom should come naturally with age, and the gradual integration of all our gifts and talents, including, as I have tried to stress in this book, our weaknesses and our woundedness. It should be a time when we have moved beyond the egoistic mindset of youthful years to allow the trials and challenges of life's journey to lead us into the bigger space, the bigger picture, the more expansive and forgiving place that we call the wisdom of the wound.

I think we Salesians sometimes struggle with the word *holy*. It can suggest a certain preciousness, a kind of detachment from life producing a rather joyless lifestyle; but when we look at the life of Jesus he doesn't live that way. It's very interesting to see how Jesus distances himself from his cousin, John the Baptist. He clearly holds him in high regard – no one born of a woman is greater than he – yet in the next breath he adds that the least in the kingdom of God is greater than John. He seems to be suggesting that John is still in some ways doing the first-half of life journey. His preaching is moralistic and certainly suggests that God wants to both reward and punish. Jesus points to his loving, compassionate, forgiving Father. At the heart of the spiritual revolution today is a return to what Jesus actually taught and in particular the fact that we come to God through our imperfections and wounds, not by moral achievements; in the end we are all saved by mercy.

We tend to think that Jesus was an ascetic, and John certainly was, but Jesus reacts to how the religious establishment of the day refused to listen to either himself and John for entirely opposite reasons:

> We played the flute for you and you did not dance; we wailed and you did not mourn. For John came neither eating nor drinking, and they say, *He has a demon*; the son of Man came eating and

> drinking, and they say, *Look, a glutton and a drunkard, a friend of tax-collectors and sinners.* Yet wisdom is vindicated by her deeds.[52]

Jesus was often seen dining with sinners and this seemed to shock both John's disciples as well as the Pharisees. His path did not involve turning his back on the world or its people, instead he offered forgiveness and fullness of life. He did this by the path of *kenosis*, a self-emptying love of engagement, of sharing in the sufferings and the joys of others. For Jesus, holiness was not about separation but participation.

When we look at Don Bosco's path to holiness it models the kenotic path of Jesus. It was not a way of penance and long practices of piety, but an invitation to the young to enjoy games, music, theatre and outings. As Don Bosco pointed out to Dominic Savio, the Salesian path was not about severe penances, but a way of cheerfulness, of tasting and the sharing of the joy of a life lived in God's love based on the family spirit. It is a life of dedicated service to others. But as Fr Eugenio Ceria points out, such a path needs careful balancing:

> People of action face two serious dangers: they are those indicated by Jesus to Martha, **who was burdened with much serving** and **anxious and worried about many things** two difficulties that can easily be found in those who are forced to divide their activity among many things. To avoid falling into this mistake we need the one thing necessary that Mary chose, and that is not to lose sight of the Lord. The centre of gravity of an active life is precisely this union with God, which prevents loss of balance or quickly restores it if lost.[53] (Author's emphasis)

What Fr Ceria is warning about, is the tendency in our Salesian spirituality to lose our balance in the face of the demands of the apostolate. Every spirituality has its shadow side and the Rector Major's warning about activism is relevant here. An activist mentality tends to embrace the Martha side of our souls and reject the Mary element. It is as if contemplation is another activity which we just can't fit into our busy schedules. Another problem arises if we read this story with

52 Mt 11:17-20

53 Eugenio Ceria *Don Bosco with God* (Paulines Publications Africa 2008) p90

our dualistic minds. We think that Jesus is criticising Martha for what she is doing. I don't think he is doing that at all. What Martha is doing is good: she is preparing a meal for Jesus, this is hospitality and it is good. The problem is that Martha is doing what she is doing out of her *false-self,* which is always judgmental and needy. She wants to perform well and be appreciated, another trait of the *false-self.* She feels rather abandoned and isolated and, in typical *false-self* fashion, she gets anxious, angry and looks for someone to blame.

In pointing to Mary's contemplative sitting, Jesus is trying to invite Martha to connect her activity with her *true-self,* which is always calm, centred and regards everything with non-judgmental compassion. Contemplation is not an add-on to our spiritual path, it is the foundation of the path. It takes us beyond the small mind of the judging *false-self* into the heart-space of compassion and forgiveness from where all authentic love emerges. It is a different way of seeing, a different way of being, and so leads to a different way of doing. This is an integrated spiritual path. In one sense it doesn't matter what we do; it is always a question of who is doing it, with us. Holiness is not an individualistic attempt to climb the ladder of perfection, but a recognition that I cannot do this alone; I have to allow Christ to do it in me. That is the path of transformation.

Presence

Salesian spirituality stresses the importance of presence, presence among the young. We are familiar with this, but the contemplative dimension uncovers another aspect of the spirituality of presence. The spiritual journey invites us to two distinct but connecting paths, the journey within and the journey without, a radical journey inward and a radical journey outward. When these come together we live what spiritual teachers call an awakened life.

Calm centring allows us to be truly present to the moment with all its imperfection and know that is how and where God loves us. Don Bosco used to say, *it is faith that does everything,* and by faith he met that trusting sense in God's abiding love for us at every moment. Mary Mazzarello was the same with her famous remark that every stitch should be done for the love of

God. For both these saints their tireless action was rooted in their deep union with God.

Jesus came to reveal the kingdom of God, but the danger of unbalanced activism is that it very quickly becomes my kingdom. That is why in describing kingdom consciousness, Jesus puts the inner attitudes firmly at the beginning of his eight Beatitudes. He starts with poverty, humility, mercy, and mourning before he gets to the call to be workers for justice and peace. The point that Jesus is making is often missed. The key to evangelising others is the recognition that we also need to be evangelised. This is a continuing and ever deepening task. In our various activities we can disguise our own dark side. Facing our dark side is the key to moving into the second-half of life. This is the agenda of the prophets, and they too, like all human beings struggled with this aspect of their calling.

The classic case is Jonah[54] who does not want the Ninevites to be converted by his preaching and literally runs away from his mission. Fleeing by ship he is thrown overboard by a frightened crew in the heat of a storm, to be swallowed by a large fish. After three days he is spat out again on dry land. He then returns to Nineveh to preach, and even then he wants God to punish them all for their sins. God provides him with a bush for shade from the heat on the hillside. When the bush withers, Jonah is angry. God replies that Jonah is far more concerned about his own shelter and protection than he is for the plight of all the people of Nineveh. The short book of only four chapters is one of the most important in the whole scripture. It portrays a prophet who is still very much stuck in the first-half of life agenda, who is still living in the *false-self,* who has not found his *true-self* that would lead him to desire mercy for the sinners of Nineveh.

We might see Jonah's story as that of a failed prophet, but when Jesus is asked for a sign that his mission is from God he replies that the only sign he will give is that of the prophet Jonah, because he underlines the great pattern of the spiritual journey that none of us can avoid, and it is this: that we don't get to God by doing it right, but by doing it wrong.

---

54 Jonah chapters 1-4

We have to die to our own image of ourselves, as working well for God, being successful in our ministry, getting people to praise us, by thinking of ourselves as in any way holy. We have to die to that small self and then rise to our true life in God. This usually happens when we experience some kind of suffering, some failure or some experience of love, or through prayer. Many of the great biblical characters such as Moses, Jacob, David, Peter and Paul, have this flawed quality. Their lives teach us that God loves imperfect people, who can move beyond the moral agenda into the fullness of grace and mercy.

If we simply stay on the level of active work, or even at the level of vocal prayer, we may get trapped by our egos which want us to stay in control, and even to control God as both Jonah and Martha wanted. It is not easy to see our own egotism. We have to step back and find a place where we can acknowledge it, own it, maybe even weep over it and see it forgiven and embraced by the mercy of God. That is the contemplative journey.

An over-worked Protestant minister came to visit Carl Jung and ask for help since he felt he was on the verge of burn-out. Jung told him to take a complete rest, but the man said that was impossible. Jung then suggested that after completing his duties for the day he should leave the evening for time to be alone, with no work. The man returned after a couple of weeks and when Jung asked him how he had spent his evening. The man replied that he had listened to music and read some books. Jung wasn't happy; he told him to do nothing, not even listen to music or read, but to sit in silence with himself. At his next appointment Jung asked him how things were, had he been able to sit in silence. The clergyman said he found it very difficult to sit in silence because he had discovered that he didn't like himself. Jung pointed out that the self he didn't like was the self he was inflicting on others in his ministry.

I think this is a very revealing story and it demonstrates why perhaps we busy Salesians don't wish to try contemplation. Because there is no doubt that we will experience both sides of ourselves: our light and our dark sides will emerge. We have already alluded to Jesus' own experience after his baptism when instead of plunging into ministry he went into the desert for forty days and nights. There, as the scriptures tell us, he met both the wild beasts and the angels. If our pastoral work is really genuine it will involve sharing the pain that others carry. Many young people carry a lot of pain these days, especially if they have been wounded by absent fathers. This is the *father wound* and is a wound shared by many young people today, not just those from poor families. To help them carry that wound and transform it, our own hearts have to be enlarged and opened to the same compassion that Jesus showed.

Jesus came to teach us the way of wisdom, a place where the opposites can be brought together. He called this place the kingdom of God; it is a place where we can learn to look at everything with non-judging compassion. That includes the failings of others as well as our own. This is what we mean today by *saving our souls*. In a sense we don't save our souls we find them, and the soul is the place of compassion that holds everything together, even our failures and our sins. The soul is the seat of contemplative wisdom. Resting in this place of compassion does not in any way take us away from active ministry. The closer we get to the heart of the divine mystery that we call God in prayer, the more we are forced outwards into compassionate action.

There is an interesting pattern in the life of the vows that shape religious life. We are emptied of our ego by our poverty which includes our faults as well as our ministry to others. As we are emptied we are filled with the love of God by the vow of chastity, the vow of love. The emptier we are, the more we can be filled by God's abundance. We then share that love with others in the place we are sent to by obedience. The cycle continues and deepens.

Holiness includes imperfection

The great shift in spirituality today is from the spirituality of perfection to the spirituality of imperfection. The rediscovery of the contemplative tradition is at the heart of this shift. The mystics have always taught this path and it is beginning to emerge into what we might call mainstream spirituality. You see it in the wisdom of Julian of Norwich who says that *first there is the fall and then the rising from the fall and both are the mercy of God.* We find it in the teaching of Jean-

Pierre de Caussade who advised a Sister, with whom he was corresponding, to rejoice every time she discovered a new imperfection. We find it in St Therese of Lisieux who claimed that even if she had every possible sin on her conscience she would lose nothing of her confidence in God's mercy in the certainty that she would be warmly received. Fr Thomas Keating, the Cistercian teacher of contemplative prayer, described that remark as one of the greatest insights of all time into the nature of God and our relationship with him. We find it in the optimistic humanism of Francis of Sales who remarks on our human failings being forgiven by God's redeeming love which embraces our imperfection and makes it more lovable than original innocence could have been. We find it in St Augustine who said, *Love and do what you will.*

I don't think we can teach this to young teenagers; they are still building their container. It is second-half of life wisdom, but in choosing Francis of Sales as our patron Don Bosco wanted us to both live our own lives and also educate the young in an atmosphere of loving-kindness rather than condemnation and criticism. In that atmosphere of joy and optimism such wisdom can eventually be learned.

Humility and Holiness

No kind of holiness is possible without humility. The author of the Cloud of Unknowing teaches that there are two kinds of humility and we need both if we are to integrate our wounds of our lives into the second-half of life so that true wisdom and compassion can emerge. The author calls them *imperfect and perfect humility.*

Healthy religion, as the prophets remind us, includes accepting our wounded human condition. None of us are perfect, none of us ever get it all together. But if that self-knowledge develops into self-loathing we are caught in a spiritual trap. This is imperfect humility and a first step in spiritual growth. Such negativity can all too easily reinforce our sense of unworthiness, a woe-is-me mentality which is self-regarding and reinforces the sense that we can never be good enough. It is true, of course, that we can never be worthy of God's love. But that is not the point! Our worthiness is a gift of grace.

Self-knowledge cannot end in the awareness of our faults and failings. It has to open into and fall into the mercy and love of God. This is the crucial insight of the saints who say that our failings are the way into God. But how can we do this? The answer is to move from self-knowledge to self-forgetfulness. The author of the Cloud of Unknowing says that we must learn to fall into the endless mercy and forgiveness of God. This is when our wounds become sacred and it seems to be the reason why the saints and mystics who know they are not perfect, still try their best to eradicate their faults, but recognise that they can never succeed fully. Mary Mazzarello certainly understood this lesson about humility. In a conference to her Sisters, she warns them against being too disappointed by their defects:

> Because that would be the greatest pride of all. Instead we must throw ourselves into Jesus' arms promising him to be more watchful so we can correct ourselves.[55]

We see the same lack of ego in Don Bosco's reply to an Oblate priest who asked how he was able to be so successful in so many demanding projects:

> Look. It has nothing to do with me! It is the Lord who does everything! When he wants to show that something is his work, he makes use of the poorest instrument. And this is what happens in my case. If he had found a poorer priest, one less worthy than me, he would have used him as his chosen instrument for that work, and let poor Don Bosco follow his natural vocation as curate in some country parish.[56]

The union with God that allowed Don Bosco and Mary Mazzarello to become active contemplatives demonstrates that contemplation and action are complementary dimensions of God's loving presence in the world. They moved beyond the ego boundaries of the *false-self* and saw themselves as humble instruments of God's grace in the world. In them, the ordinary events of life became transformed into manifestations of God's loving delight in our broken world. Their compassion and loving-kindness reached out to embrace the vulnerability of

---

55 Quoted by Carlo Colli *The Spirit of Mornese* (Don Bosco Publications New Rochelle NY 1982) p86

56 Quoted in Eugenio Ceria *Don Bosco with God* (Paulines Publications, Africa 2008) p72

all that is lost and broken not just in the young and the poor but also in us. Their action was always united to the source of God's abiding love in that secret place where God dwells within us. Like them we are called to surrender to that flow of love that includes all things with non-judgmental compassion.

Being human means to be imperfect, to be limited, to need to grow. Mature spirituality gives us the ability to live joyfully in an imperfect world and this matters because an imperfect world is all we have got and God seems happy to use our very imperfection to teach us how to make the journey with forgiving love.

Chapter 10 – Mystics and Prophets

> In a time of fragmentation and fragility, like our own, it is necessary to overcome the dissipation of energy in hyperactivity and cultivate the unity of a spiritual life through the acquisition of a profound sense of the mystical dimension and a sound asceticism. This nourishes apostolic commitment and guarantees an effective ministry.[57]
>
> We commit ourselves to enhance the prophetic and mystical dimensions of our vocation in our communities, vitally assuming the educational spirituality of Don Bosco and Mary Mazzarello.[58]

To live the second-half of life is to find the real goal of life. We can begin to taste what the first-half of life helped to contain and foster. Any growth in spiritual maturity needs to *tanscend* and *include*. A move to non-dual thinking must also include dualistic thinking. A balanced life requires both, but as we mature we learn to place our dualistic judgements inside the bigger space of the non-dual mind. We discover in contemplative prayer that our thoughts are not our enemies, we do have to make judgements; but in the second-half of life these judgements come from a place of wisdom and compassion, the place of loving-kindness. Some might argue that this lacks realism, it suggests that spirituality is soft and mushy; life is not simple and sometimes tough choices have to be made.

That is why it is so important to make the transition well. We do this when we own our woundedness. All classic stories lead the hero or heroine into a fall, into some experience of suffering and failure, and this is necessary for them to achieve wisdom. This distinguishes authentic prophecy from what might be termed soft religion. The current sexual abuse crisis has revealed a gaping wound in the heart of the Church and its hierarchical structure. Many Church leaders did not know

---

57 Pope Benedict XVI *Message to Salesians*, (*General Chapter 26*, Rome 2008)

58 FMA *Chapter Resolution* (*General Chapter 22*, Rome 2008)

how to acknowledge this wound and the cover up has done great damage to the Church. At the same time there seem to be many who favour a return to a more conservative Church, even to rolling back the reforms and spirit of Vatican II, as we reach its fiftieth anniversary. The recent top down imposition of the new English translation of the liturgical texts has caused widespread distress and dismay. The Church seems to be looking for loyal soldiers who are trained in blind acceptance of commands. Loyal soldiers are products of the first-half of life. We all have a loyal soldier inside us to help negotiate the first-half of life, but the soldier needs to be discharged if we are to grow into mature spirituality.

The Western World is suffering from a leadership problem. Many institutions have failed us: not just Church leaders and priests, but politicians, bankers, the police, journalists and so on. Poll results often show a serious loss of trust in such established leaders. It is the military who often top the polls in public esteem. This is significant and it confirms Bill Plotkins' view that much of our world is stuck at the egocentric first stage of life. In a time of cultural stability this might go unnoticed. In times of profound and rapid change such as ours it no longer works. In religious life, and at the highest level of the Church, our leaders are thankfully pointing this out. In writing this book, I have been struck by the number of quotations I have found calling us as Salesians to live as active contemplatives. The quotes are all there from Don Bosco himself, to the SDB Constitutions, the FMA Constitutions, from Rectors Major, Mothers General, and from both SDB and FMA Chapters. We have received a similar message from both Pope John Paul II and Pope Benedict XVI, such as the words at the head of this chapter.

I'm not sure if we will ever return to the high numbers of religious and priestly vocations that we enjoyed in the last century, when we religious became a large – often underpaid – workforce in the Church. I came into religious life at the time of Vatican II when that model of religious life was still the norm, and we were formed not to ask too many questions – preferably none at all – and to get on with the work. Fortunately Vatican II began to permeate religious life with its stress on the dignity of the person built around the idea of dialogue and the summons to the renewal of religious life. But despite all the renewed formation courses in psychology, sociology, and theology there was something missing from our novitiates and formation programmes, and it seems to have been missing in most, if not all, other religious orders, congregations and seminaries. Nobody was teaching and encouraging contemplative prayer. We were all taught just to meditate, and while I have no doubt that both Don Bosco and Mary Mazzarello lived in deep union with God they did not teach contemplation to their followers. Len Kofler makes the point well when he says that if we are going to teach the mystical path we need teachers who are making the journey themselves.[59] The task of the second-half of life is to pass on wisdom to the next generation. This is both a personal and a collective task. My own view is that this is a key task for the flourishing of religious life in the future.

The advice to live more reflective lives is coming thick and fast these days from our superiors and our Chapter documents. In May 2010, the union of Superiors General met in Rome to discuss the theme *The Future of Religious Life lies in the strength of its mysticism and its prophecy.* They urge us to a more integrated spirituality, one that includes both action and contemplation. They point out the danger of living an unbalanced life, an unconscious life, an unawakened life. Religious life is not primarily a workforce for the Church; its purpose is to live intensely the witness of the Gospel for the times in which we are living. It is a liminal group in society, a charismatic lifestyle, and because we are between stories of the old and the new today, this is not an easy place to be. Our highly extraverted and busy Western world needs to recover its soul. Nowhere in the Gospel does Jesus ask us to become workaholics. If we want to give ourselves a task and challenge today as religious, it is not to pile activity on to activity but to balance that activity with a more reflective life. It is not just about being prophets, it is becoming both prophets and mystics.

In his commentary of the Strenna for 2012, the Rector Major, Fr Chávez, called on us to *re-interpret the Preventive System*

59 Len Kofler *Formation Today* (The Furrow Trust Maynooth, Ireland 2011) p293-295

in contemporary terms.[60] This is the way to keep Don Bosco's dream alive for our times. Our troubled times desperately need a new vision. This is the challenge that we face in this moment in history. I think that the spirituality for the two halves of life can help towards this re-interpretation. Mature spirituality includes both the first and second-half of life. In our Salesian Preventive System we are asked to include reason, prophecy and mysticism. If we throw ourselves into compassionate living without having compassion for ourselves we will end up exhausted and burned out. When our British Salesian province went into Liberia in West Africa I remember the wise words of Archbishop Michael Francis:

> You cannot live exactly like the local people. You have to have clean water, you have to take care of yourselves, to avoid getting sick.

This is reason and good sense speaking, and it is necessary to temper an excess of caring. To know when to care and not to care is true wisdom.

That is why the prophetic mission of Jesus to the poor and needy was rooted in his mystical life. He is constantly withdrawing from the crowd, even from his disciples sometimes, to be in communion with his *Abba, Father.* This intimacy was at the heart of everything that he did. He lived an intense contemplative life, sometimes spending whole nights in prayer. We are not being asked to do that but the essential pattern is clear. If we are going to be prophets to our world today we have to be mystics. There has to be some inner experiential knowledge of God.

Mysticism is Ordinary

We have nearly all been educated to believe that mysticism involves dramatic visions and ecstasies. We can read stories about characters such as St Joseph Cupertino who used to levitate when praying and float around the chapel. Teresa of Avila is noted for her ecstatic visions, but such people fall into the category of the 5% who experienced what Carmelite Ruth Burrows calls lights-on mysticism. For the other 95% it is

60 Fr Pascual Chávez *Acts of the General Council* (Jan-April 2012) p28

usually lights-off! Part of the wisdom of Centering Prayer is the advice not to cling to any *vision* that might occur during silent prayer time.

The point of mysticism is to remind us of our true identity and to get us grounded in reality. The mystics are those people whose lives have been transformed so that they are one with God, one with other people, and one with creation. This oneness is true of all of us; the problem is that we are not aware of it. Thomas Keating describes original sin as coming to full reflective self-consciousness without the certitude of personal union with God. This is why reflective living is so important and necessary for our growth. Back in the fourth century, Gregory of Nyssa said that sin is *refusing to grow*. This is what Jesus meant in his gentle correcting of Martha when he said there is really *only one thing necessary*. We have to become aware of our *true-self* and overcome the sense of separation from God. We have to allow the flow of divine love to flow through us so that all our activity is bathed in this love. This is the union of action and contemplation. It is the discovery – which is always a gift of grace – that God and our *true-self* are not different. We are not God, but we are not separate from God. If we can believe this, it changes everything. Our lives are filled with a deep joy, peace and happiness that no one can take away. We see this serenity and joy clearly in the lives of both Don Bosco and Mary Mazzarello.

Original sin is not the result of personal wrong doing on our part, but its presence in our lives reveals the human condition as imperfect, flawed and full of contradictions. It accounts for the sense of alienation, estrangement and forgetfulness in our relationship with God. A regular practice of contemplative prayer opens us to our existential poverty and need in the presence of God. We discover that we don't know how to pray. We seem to fail every time. Our egos think we have to succeed and will urge us to give up, but gradually we fall into the great paradox that Jesus teaches: that the poor are blessed with the gift of the kingdom. Our emptiness is filled with God's unconditional love, and the gifts of the Spirit are awakened in our lives: joy, peace, compassion, forgiveness, mercy, and love. Of course we all slip back into forgetfulness, but the regular daily practice of contemplative prayer brings us back to the place of oneness, even during our busy active lives. There is a price, of course, for this unitive consciousness: the grain of wheat has to fall into the ground and die. Jesus tells us that we have to lose our *false-self* and fall into our *true-self*. This is the death of the ego and it is not easy. It is only love, suffering or prayer that gets us there.

Prophecy and Mysticism

Hans Urs Von Balthassar, a theologian, teaches that the most important word in Catholic spirituality is the word *and*. Healthy spirituality is always *both/and* rather than *either/or*. This confirms the crucial linkage between prophecy and mysticism. There are many people in our world who critique the injustices in our societies, who want to speak on behalf of the poor and the needy. This is clearly a good thing, but too often this criticism comes out of the dualistic mind and it simply creates opposition. The dualistic binary mind can't get to unity. We see it in so many discussions with our well-educated politicians who can't get beyond the dualistic mind. It can't help splitting and dividing the field into winners and losers, right and wrong, good or bad. As we saw in chapter five, it is the wrong operating system. While it is so useful in ordinary everyday tasks it cannot reach what the mystics call the unified field of unitive consciousness, or seeing with the heart, or the kingdom of God as Jesus called it.

The words of Fr Viganò, quoted at the beginning of the Introduction, that we are *with Don Bosco and the times not with the times of Don Bosco*, are very relevant here. We seem to have reached an evolutionary point in our history when more and more people are searching and hungry for a spirituality that goes beyond the simplistic *either/or* judgements and touches the deeper place of the heart, not as the seat of our emotions, but as an organ of perception, a way of seeing reality. This allows us to critique injustice from a different place. I don't think this means that we will never become angry at the injustices of our world: the child trafficking, the use of boy soldiers, the exploitation of women, the use of violence, the rejection of those who are different such as homosexuals or those of another religion. If we are to be prophets in our time we have to feel the pain of all of this, but what mysticism teaches, is that we are part of the pain also. Our lives also are full of imperfection and contradiction. So our righteous anger has to be tempered by non-judgmental compassion. We can't live in a nice mystical bubble, oblivious to the sufferings of others; we have to learn how to carry our own pain alongside the pain of the world. As Richard Rohr teaches, if we don't transform our pain, we will transmit it. We see so much evidence of this in our world today.

The mystery of the Cross is the place where prophecy and mysticism meet. Jesus takes the pain of the world into himself and transforms it into forgiveness.

Sacred and Secular

Our atonement theories have taught that Jesus became human to die for us on the Cross to satisfy his Father's wrath. I much prefer the teaching of Duns Scotus and Francis of Sales that Jesus is the purpose and high point of creation. He is the blueprint we are called to follow and imitate. We will see more of this in the next chapter in looking at the Cosmic Christ. Jesus became human to show us how to put the opposites together: heaven and earth, light and dark, matter and spirit, body and soul, sacred and secular. He becomes the reconciling third that holds all the opposites together. When he dies on the Cross the Gospel of Mark tells us that *the veil of the temple was torn in two from top to bottom.*[61]

This is a very striking image because the temple was known as the *fanum*, the holy place. Anything outside the temple was *pro fanum*, beyond the holy, the profane. Our dualistic minds have seized on this split between the secular world and the holy world. It partly accounts for the split in the history of Christian spirituality that divides contemplation from action. It has led to the kind of problems in our understanding of sexuality as we saw in a previous chapter. Having declared that we have all been created in the image and likeness of God the penny catechism asked the question, *Is this likeness found chiefly in the body or the soul?* We have all suffered from the answer that was given to us.

61 Mk 15.37

The same dualistic thinking sets up another false division between prayer and work. Reducing prayer to *saying prayers* actually misrepresents God. He is imaged as a remote figure up there in heaven who has to decide between the endless requests he gets from us: some of us pray for fine weather while others pray for rain and we are all familiar with the sports fans who pray to God for a victory for their team. Even science today is teaching us that matter and spirit cannot be divided. God is not out there on a cloud observing us from above, marking all our faults and failings like a driving instructor. God is present in the deepest part of our being. As Mother General Yvonne Reungoat FMA says, *mysticism makes us good from within.*[62]

God is the energy (love) that is at the heart of all creation, the Spirit that drives us on to build the Kingdom here on earth. Prayer is not just another duty that we have to perform to keep God happy; it is the very energy of our souls that wants to burst forth into creative loving action in the world. Prayer is who we are. Karl Rahner says that we are *pressured* from within to evolve. That pressure is the Holy Spirit, the Loving Energy that wants to become present in us. This is why we have been created. Prayer and action are two sides of the same coin. The mystics need to become prophets (and the best clearly are) and the prophets need to become mystics. Prayer is allowing God's love for the world, and especially for the poor and the needy, to come alive in our hearts so that it can spill over into our everyday calculating minds and change the way they see reality. Instead of noticing differences and judging them we see the underlying unity and connection in all beings and all Being, and learn to celebrate the differences.

Being Mirrored

In the journey of life we all begin with the field of action. What do I have to do to respond to what God is asking from me and how do I do it? We learn, experiment, try our best and we fail. This is good and necessary action. In the second-half of life we move to a deeper more personal question: *Who are you God?* and *Who am I?* It's a more relational question and it moves us

62 Circular letter *Holiness, the Secret of the Institute's Fruitfulness* (Rome Sept 2011)

from process to content. Instead of trying to impress God with our efforts we move to a more direct enjoyment of God's love.

If we are to mature in life we all need to be mirrored by someone who accepts and loves us for what we are rather than what we do. This is the heart of Don Bosco's Preventive System. If we are not properly gazed at by loving parents we tend to look for ways to demonstrate our worthiness. Again this is a necessary stage and we need to prove our love especially to our fathers and male leaders, teachers, coaches, etc. With God, however, the relationship is much more intimate. It is a much more maternal gaze of unconditional love. If we can negotiate the transitional path of dying to the ego that wants to go on feeling worthy we can fall into the abyss of this love. Some young people experience this early in life, such as Dominic Savio, Laura Vicuna or Therese of Lisieux, or children that cope with illnesses such as cancer. For most of us it takes time and as we grow in years our contemplative soul begins to awaken and calls us home. That is the call of the Spirit and we cannot control it or make it happen. But if we have been well mentored by compassionate and wise adults we are best placed to surrender to it. Where our egos seek control and security, our souls are happy to be embraced by Holy Mystery. The healthy mirroring by our parents, teachers and others gives way to the experience of being mirrored by an Absolute Love. This is the content of the spiritual journey, the enjoyment of the Treasure Within, the Pearl of Great Price, the Holy Mystery. At this point we no longer see any real distinction between action and contemplation. It is all one flow.

We have fallen through our very limited egoic point of view and we no longer have to work everything out or to achieve everything. We learn to live with unknowing as well as knowing. Our reason gives way to love. We are in the kingdom of God, and it is not something we have achieved. We can look back at our many failures and wrong turnings and know that, as the writer of Ephesians says, *We are God's work of art.* Now our prayer and our work can become more like a seamless garment. We have discovered what Fr Chávez calls *the profoundly mystical nature of our mission.*[63]

63 Fr Pascual Chávez *Acts of the General Council* (May-August 2011) p23

The prophets remind us that the fullness of the kingdom is not yet present in the world and we commit ourselves to realising its presence wherever we are. The mystic reminds us that the gift is already given, that in this ordinary moment God is fully present. If we are to bring about God's kingdom – and not our own – we need to rest in the delight of what is given to us in each moment. As Thomas Merton says, *we are already one but we think that we are not.*

Chapter 11 – The Evolving Dream

> This is the real revolution that Don Bosco and Mary Mazzarello understood and put into practice, living with love, as contemplatives, in the reality of every day.[64]
>
> We are constantly busy, even our leisure time is ruled by the clock. We flit from activity to activity, seldom absorbed in one thing for long before we are thinking about what we have to do next. But if you are to get to the heart of things, contemplation is called for.[65]

Living in liminal times is not easy but I am suggesting that this is the reality of our times. We can look back on the world of modernity with its excessive reliance on rationality and its dualisms with a mixture of nostalgia and relief, and we look to the future with a mixture of anxiety and excitement. Many today are suggesting that a new consciousness is at the heart of this radical change. As we survey the wreckage of environmental disasters, of violence and war, of the collapse of the banking system, the bankruptcy of whole countries, we feel the call for something more meaningful and creative, the need for us all to work together for the good of humanity. The saints and mystics have always known and spoken of the experience of oneness, of the unity of humanity, and today our scientists are confirming that this sense of unity and connectedness extends to all of creation.

We know that Don Bosco's vocational dream at the age of nine was repeated at different stages of his life. Sometime between 1871 and 1872 he experienced a new phase of this dream as he saw his Salesians evangelising bands of native tribesmen in distant lands. It marked the re-birth for Don Bosco of his youthful desire to become a missionary in foreign lands. Now, in the second-half of his life, he was able to send his Salesians, to be followed shortly by Salesian Sisters, to the missions. Today this dream of Don Bosco continues to evolve. As we find ourselves in an increasingly globalised world we are beginning

64 Mother Yvonne Reungoat FMA, *Closing Address* (General Chapter 22, Rome 2008)
65 John Feehan, *The Singing Heart of the World* (Columba Press, Dublin 2011) p119

to see the need for a globalised spirituality that embraces not just our world but the whole of creation.

A particular feature of our times is the coming together of two old foes, science and religion, that have really been at odds since the beginning of the scientific revolution. This would not be true of all scientists, nor of all believers, but as science is uncovering more and more of the story of the universe, what is called *deep time* is being revealed as a profound mystery that embraces all of us. The transformation brought about by the discoveries of Einstein and the work of quantum physicists is breathtaking in its scope and vastness. Don Bosco and Mary Mazzarello lived in a very different age, but they certainly felt this connection through the contemplative eyes with which they viewed the world.

We all know of the contemplative experience of the young Mary gazing towards the parish church through the window at Valponasca. It is interesting also to note the memory of Don Rua who knew Don Bosco so well:

> Sometimes when I accompanied him as he went to rest late at night, he would stop to contemplate the starry sky and remain there, forgetful of his tiredness, talking about the immensity, omnipotence and wisdom of God. On other occasions in the countryside he would point out to us the beauty of the fields, or the abundance and richness of the fruit, and this led to a conversation about God's goodness and providence.[66]

Having been raised in the countryside, Don Bosco had a heart and soul attuned to the beauty and grandeur of God's creation. The growth of towns and cities has made this appreciation more difficult for us, but young people have a real concern over how our plundering of the earth is affecting their future. As words such as *non-violent* and *non-dual* are entering into mainstream spirituality, so too are words such as *ecology* and *biodiversity*. Living the dream of Don Bosco today for the benefit of our young people involves an increasing awareness of how the Universe Story and the Christian Story can converge because that seems to be part of God's Dream for our times.

---

66 Don Rua quoted in Eugenio Ceria, *Don Bosco with God* (Paulines Publications Kenya, Africa 2008) p69

We are clearly living in an evolving universe and humanity has a crucial role in saying *yes* or *no* as new patterns emerge.

An Evolving Universe

The people of the bible lived in a three-tier universe, with God up there in the sky, Hades, the shadowy land of the dead, beneath the flat earth on which humans lived. This world-view was later replaced by the Ptolemaic system of a concentric universe with everything centred on human life. Centuries later, Isaac Newton described the universe as a machine with very fixed laws. Today we have learned that we live in an evolving cosmos which began to emerge 13.7 billion years ago. The whole story is an unfolding one, opening out its narrative all the way, and the key is the movement from simple to more complex structures. Our science reveals how large and spacious the cosmos is: our Milky Way is just one of 100 billion galaxies, consisting of 100 billion stars stretching 100,000 light years in diameter. We are clearly not the centre of the universe as we naively thought in the past. Everything, including ourselves, has emerged from the Big Bang which in fact was a tiny microscopic event which has continued to balloon in what the Hubble telescope reveals is an expanding universe.

This amazing story is a humbling one as we view the shortness of not only our individual lives, but also our collective story as a species. After billions of years of inert, dead matter, the first stars appeared ten billion years ago. Our sun was born four and half billion years ago, and the solar system half a billion years after that, followed by the emergence of the earth. With the development of plant and animal life, our first ancestors started to emerge around four million years ago as *Homo erectus* and evolved into *Homo sapiens*, around three million years ago. Our immediate ancestors arrived, about half a million years ago.[67] The development has been from matter to increasing consciousness, and each crucial stage in the process is marked by a quantum leap of consciousness. In an emerging universe something new arises out of a previous life form. Today, we know ourselves as material beings who

67 See Judy Cannato, *Fields of Compassion* (Sorin Books, Notre Dame Indiana USA 2010)

are also spiritual beings, beings with consciousness. We can begin to comprehend the holy mystery that we are part of and have emerged from. Our lives may be humbled by the vastness of the creation story but we recognise that we are a crucial part of the mystery. The universe has become conscious in us, and this consciousness, this emerging spirit, has been in some miraculous and mysterious way present from the very beginning. In this new understanding, we can no longer rely on tribal or ethnocentric consciousness.

A Mystery of Participation

What this story teaches us is that we are a small but conscious part of a much larger mystery of life and death in which we all participate. Even Stone-Age men and women had a sense of a transcendent mystery, that they were – as we are – contingent beings, dependent on some kind of Absolute. This sense of the transcendent dimension of life is what we call the *Holy* or the *Sacred.* They might have experienced it in nature, or in thunder or lightning, or the sun and the moon. As humanity grew in consciousness we discovered a desire to communicate with this Sacred Mystery with special rituals and ceremonies. In what has been called the Axial Age from 800-200 BCE all the great religions emerged, as did the sense of ourselves as individual subjects.

Owen Barfield[68] called this stage *Original Participation* when humans knew the holy through experiences of nature, art, dance, music and painting. They were participating, at a simple but real level, in what Thomas Merton later called *the cosmic dance of creation.* It is an essentially relational mystery and we are all part of it. Barfield says that when Jesus appeared he offered us Full and Final Participation. He shows us how to put the human and the divine together, to put matter and spirit together, to bring all things together in unity, everything in heaven and everything on earth as we read in the letter to the Ephesians. To accept the message of Jesus is to see the fundamental unity of all things. The Incarnation was always in the mind of God from the very beginning and God gave us

---

68 Owen Barfield, *Saving the Appearances: A Study in idolatry* (New York: Harcourt Brace 1957)

Jesus so we could see the Holy Mystery in human form.

Our egoic consciousness has been trained to think in terms of separation and division, and, as mentioned earlier, in the last five hundred years or so since the Reformation and the Enlightenment we have been living in what Owen Barfield calls the *Desert of Non-Participation.* This is the period when the contemplative tradition was largely lost in the Christian Church. Today as our scientists reveal more and more of our evolving universe we see that unity and connection is the great pattern and our task, as human beings, is to participate in this mystery, to allow it to unfold in us and to honour it in creation as well as in each other. This is the great web of life, the great web of meaning.

If Jesus shows us how to put matter and spirit together, we are called to do the same as members of the Body of Christ. At this point in our history we are being summoned to a new consciousness. To use the word *we* today has to include the *we* of other religions, even the *we* of unbelievers and the *we* of creation. As we *tanscend* and include, we respect and cherish all that our faith tradition has taught us in the first-half of life. As we move into the second-half of life, which always involves embracing the Bigger Picture, the Bigger Story, we can see a new dream emerging for humanity, faithful to the prayer of Jesus – *that all may be one.* An evolutionary spirituality can allow new things to emerge, something more than the previous stage although not entirely different.

Ken Wilber says that we are holons. We are a whole that is a part of other holons in the sense that a whole atom is a part of a whole molecule, and a whole molecule is part of a whole cell, and a whole cell is part of a whole organism. So we learn to see ourselves as part of natural families, of local communities, of religious communities, of nations, of membership of the human race. Without such growth in vision we are trapped to repeat the mistakes of racism and terrorism and war. We Salesians have to educate our young people into this new consciousness so that they can see beyond divisions and glimpse the underlying unity. In my own experience, of working with asylum seekers, I have been in many schools where the children tend to have an antagonistic view towards refugees. Not surprisingly they feel threatened by people who are different. Once they meet a refugee and listen to their story they can get a sense that what human beings have in common is more important than what divides them – that we are all created to live in peace, to welcome diversity rather than feel threatened by it, because God the Creator clearly loves diversity.

This is the sense of kinship that all religions honour when they ask their followers *to welcome the stranger*, as Jesus himself clearly does. This sense of kinship is a spiritual sense, and it is developed by an education that broadens out to embrace the vastness of the universe and the discovery that we are, in fact, all related genetically: all mankind is one family. The Incarnation reveals that God is at the heart of this emerging universe, that the energy that flows through all things and all people is, in fact, the Spirit of God. Jesus is God's visual aid for this reality flowing through himself. In his knowledge of himself as Son of the Father and Son of Man he reveals the beginning and the end of the Creation Story. He invites us to share God's dream for humanity with him as we discover and accept that we too have the divine DNA in our very humanity, created as we are in the image and likeness of God.

The Cosmic Christ

We know from the story of Jesus that people of his time were largely unable to accept such a high level of consciousness, and this has remained true throughout history, during which we Christians have made steps both forward and backwards in religious consciousness. In Jesus, we see the perfect fit between God's offer of unconditional love and grace, and humanity's acceptance of that offer. We know from our own spiritual journey that we struggle to live at that level. We fail and lapse back into our egotistic point of view, but an evolutionary spirituality teaches us that this woundedness is built into the pattern of creation. Our Universe Story teaches us that nothing will last for ever, that everything changes, even our sun will die. The Church calls this the Paschal Mystery and Jesus himself goes through this process in his death and Resurrection. The rhythm of dying and rising is built into the Creation Story. As human beings we have the capacity to say yes or no to this pattern. Thomas Berry points out that in these liminal times we are living between these two stories, the story of science and the story of religion and we have to become part of the emerging story in which the two converge. That is why we feel a sense of dislocation; religious people keep asking, *Where are all the young people?*

Perhaps the first great Christian to grasp this vision in our times was the Jesuit scientist and palaeontologist, Pierre Teilhard de Chardin, whose writings in his own time were so challenging to religious leaders that none of them were published. That has since changed, and both John Paul II and Pope Benedict XVI have quoted him in recent years. Teilhard saw the figure of Christ as the connection between the two great stories. The whole of the evolutionary pattern is visible in Christ who emptied himself (*kenosis*) from Godhead to assume our human flesh and all the limitations that involved. We Christians need reminding at times that Christ was not the last name of Jesus. Christ is the title of the Risen One who has passed through the mystery of death to the fullness of Risen life. As a human being Jesus is the prototype and blueprint of everything that God is doing in creation. God is love, and creation reflects his desire for a lover, someone who could receive this unconditional love and give it back. In Jesus, this love breaks through in a completely new way; he is totally receptive to the grace and love of the God he called Father. He receives the radiant love of God completely and invites all of us to do the same. Although his mission was initially to the Jewish people he very quickly demonstrates the inclusive nature of God's love; this radiant presence embraces all that is, and every little piece of the universe is sustained by this powerful energy, which is light and love.

This insight fired the imagination of Teilhard de Chardin who discerned God's emerging love and creative power at the heart of our evolving universe. He spoke of the sacredness of matter as well as spirit, modelled in the flesh and soul of Jesus. He understood Paul's description of the whole of creation groaning in one great act of giving birth. If the first Axial age saw the birth of the great religions, and the second Axial age saw the birth of science and technology, he foresaw, as many others have agreed, that we are on the edge of a new phase of planetary awareness. This is the Story we have to pass on to the upcoming generation. But it requires our conscious participation. This is where our culture needs healing.

The spiritual journey confronts us with our own personal woundedness. With God's grace, the wound can be integrated into compassionate love. In contemplative, non-dual consciousness, we feel the pain of the world and of the culture we live in. Today many people experience fragmentation, and a big part of the healing process will be in the convergence of the two Great Stories, of science and spirituality, of matter and spirit, of prophecy and mysticism. Teilhard de Chardin taught that this evolutionary movement is progressing towards the Risen Christ as the Omega point. Cosmogenesis becomes Christogenesis.

Action and Contemplation

During the twentieth century a number of mystics appeared who have revived the contemplative tradition for our times. We are emerging from *the desert of non-participation.* Scientists are speaking like mystics as they see how unknowable the quantum universe really is. Mystics are teaching scientists a more contemplative way of seeing. As the Universe story and the Christian story begin to converge we are given an opportunity and a challenge to unite both stories as a dynamic and creative impulse at the heart of creation. In Christ we are discovering ourselves as both the Universe Story and the Christian story. Both stories are about connectedness, as we see the fundamental unity of all things and their rich diversity at the same time. We can understand contemplation not just as an optional extra, but a crucial key to seeing things and people as they really are. If the whole of creation is evolving into the Omega point that is the Cosmic Christ, then we begin to see action and contemplation not as alternatives but as the *both/and* quality of a new way of being.

As we strive to build the kingdom with our creative action in the world we are learning a new rhythm of inward and outward spirituality in which action flows from the centre of our being and from there flows back in to loving action. If we Salesians can become contemplatives in action, as our Constitutions explicitly state, we can bring a unified vision and practice into contemporary spirituality. Traditionally spiritual writers have tended to see a division between loving God and loving the world. Sometimes even some of our liturgical prayers at Mass reflect this dualism as we are exhorted to love the things of heaven rather than the things of earth. We have often been told to love God and hate the world. Contemporary mystics such as Teilhard de Chardin, Thomas Merton and Karl Rahner have sought to bridge that gap. I think that successive Rector Majors have asked us Salesians to do the same as they warn us about the dangers of excessive activism divorced from an authentic inner experience of prayer. We don't bring an absent God to the people we minister to, nor do we bring an absent God to the planet on which we all live. It is hard to speak of God to others if we have not experienced God's presence in the core of our own being.

If we can connect the historical Jesus with the Risen Body of the Cosmic Christ, we can live the dream that Jesus gave us in the kingdom of God. If we can see how the mystery of God's continuous grace is constantly being given to everything in creation we can move beyond the dualism of sacred and secular to see every action as being done *in Christ* as Paul describes life in the mystical body.

We tend to see the word *mystical* as a rather vague pious word. In fact, for Paul and for Teilhard de Chardin, the word *mystical* is not just poetic language but a real description of how deeply matter and spirit are joined. Whether we eat or drink, whatever we do, is done in Christ. Every action can be divinised. If we are indeed living a mystery of participation which is a sharing in the life of the Trinity, there is no action we can do that is not an interaction. Buddhist mystic Thich Nhat Hanh says that every time he sees the page of a book he sees a cloud. Because the clouds produce the rain that waters the trees that provide the paper on which the book is written. This is contemplative seeing. Every time we breathe in and out we are interacting with the atmosphere around us. Every time we eat food we are part of a long chain of connection involving the earth, the climate, and other human beings that allow this food to grow and nourish our bodies.

Salesian spirituality makes the ordinary into the extraordinary. Sometimes we see work with the young as the place where it all happens, but in a contemplative seeing, everything is included in what Teilhard called the *divine milieu*: taking a shower, reading a paper, phoning a friend, sharing a meal, telling jokes, listening to music, watching a football game. So when we interact with people during the day, we do it with a smile and a friendly interest

Such conscious living is the fruit of contemplative seeing. It teaches us humility and a deep gratitude for the gracious God who gives himself so generously. We begin to see in fact that each created thing and each human person is, in fact, the generosity of God made visible. In contemplation, we learn to connect with that Invisible Formless Being that we call God, and in our action we learn to bless the countless diverse ways in which this Invisible Source of Love is continuously manifested in every moment and in every place. We start to realise that it is not up to little old me to save the world by my ceaseless activity, but that I am a small, yet significant part of the total mystery that is the cosmic Christ. It is not so much what I do that matters but who is doing it with me and in me. This is the marriage of contemplation and action. As our world marvels in the technological breakthroughs that happen almost every day and we sometimes feel swamped by the sheer volume of information available to us, we discern the need for an inner ecology of soul that connects us with the Wisdom and Love that is at the heart of our evolving world.

Teilhard de Chardin, who was sent to China in 1923, found himself living in a tent in the Ordos desert and unable to celebrate Mass. He composed a very poetic Mass of the World in which he describes his mystical vision at the heart of all creation, a place of deep communion.

On the occasion of his priestly jubilee Pope John Paul II describes his own ministry in similar words:

> I have been able to celebrate Holy Mass in chapels built along mountain paths, on lakeshores and sea coasts: I have celebrated it on altars built in stadiums and in city squares. This varied scenario of celebrations of the Eucharist has given me a

> powerful experience of its universal and, so to speak, cosmic character. Yes Cosmic! Because even when it is celebrated on the humble altar of a country church, the Eucharist is always in some way celebrated on the altar of the world. It unites heaven and earth. It embraces and permeates all creation. The Son of God became man in order to restore all creation, in one supreme act of praise, to the One who made it out of nothing.[69]

We are often warned today about the split between the sacred and the secular. The sacred is already in the secular for those who have eyes to see. That is the oneness that the mystics enjoy.

69 John Paul II *Ecclesia de Eucharistia*, par 8 quoted in Hugh O'Donnell *Eucharist and the Living Earth* (Columba Press, Dublin, Ireland, 2012) p27-28

Chapter 12 – Mary and the Sacred Feminine

> His mother treasured all these things in her heart.[70]

> Doing has taken precedence over being; but is it right to give priority to the work of our own hands rather than to God's will for each of us? [71]

> The future of the charism does not depend on the growth of the works as much as the growth of the person.[72]

There are many voices today speaking about the emergence of the sacred feminine. The first-half of life's journey is dominated by masculine values such as law and order, rules and regulations, morality, hierarchy, separateness and boundaries. The second-half of life is more of an invitation to wisdom, to creating communion, learning to live with paradoxes and contradictions, and how to hold opposites together with compassion, loving-kindness and forgiveness, virtues more associated with the feminine. This is not an *either/or* issue: each one of us has to integrate the masculine and the feminine into our personal growth. A mature society and culture faces the same challenge. Many spiritual teachers are saying that we are still heavily weighted in favour of masculine values.

From the very beginning, from Don Bosco's boyhood dream, the Salesian story has been rooted in the maternal protection and guidance of Mary, the Mother of God. In the early years of his ministry Don Bosco's devotion to Mary was to Our Lady of Consolation. He was obviously attracted to the idea of Mary's consoling presence in the lives of his boys. It was in the church dedicated to Mary under that title that the boys of the Oratory set up their vigil of prayer when Don Bosco was seriously ill in 1846. After the definition of the Dogma of the Immaculate Conception by Pius IX in 1854, he began to favour this title more, and he underlined how so many significant events, such as the foundational event with Bartholomew Garelli, occurred on December 8th, the feast of Mary Immaculate.

---

70 Lk 2:51

71 Fr Pascual Chávez *Acts of the General Council* (July-September 2003) p21

72 Mother Yvonne Reungoat *Circular Letter* (Rome July 24th 2011)

Salesian historians Francis Desramaut and Arthur Lenti agree that Don Bosco's views on the society of his time were politically and morally conservative. His devotion to Mary, Help of Christians, also fitted into his conservative frame of mind. He was not comfortable with the liberal political agenda of his time. His understanding of religion, of scripture, ecclesiology, and other religions also reflected this traditional frame of mind. But as Fr Viganò and Fr Chávez have reminded us our task is not to slavishly imitate Don Bosco but to take his charism and his spirituality and live it in today's world. As we have seen, this is a world of profound and radical change, very much an evolving world. Just to imitate everything that Don Bosco said and did would kill the dream of Don Bosco; we are called to live the evolving dream in the challenging times in which we find ourselves. Article 17 of our SDB Constitutions makes it very clear that the Salesian does not bewail his own times.

My point, in this short book, is to say that we are on the edge of a very profound spiritual change in our times, a spiritual revolution that is only just beginning. I believe that the Holy Spirit is bringing about a deep change in our inner selves, the breaking-in of a new consciousness that is moving us out of our sense of ourselves as individual autonomous egos into a new vision more open to the essential oneness of all things. This does not destroy our individuality but enhances our personal growth and maturity through healthy relatedness. It gives rise to a spirituality of communion, of presence, of awareness and it provides a new way of seeing. In the first-half of life we tend to focus on measuring and controlling reality. We learn facts, build up knowledge, and we develop our analytical reasoning power. The trouble is that this in many ways reinforces the ego, but it is a necessary stage and foundational stage. It builds the container. We all need a healthy ego. But we also have to learn how to taste the contents of the container, and that can only happen when our narrow individual way of looking at reality dies and we are literally *born again* as Jesus says, and we begin to live as new creations. This is transformation. We move from the narrow perspective of the judging mind to the Bigger Picture, the Great Love, as we begin to see everything with the eyes of the heart, with non-judgmental compassion. This is the journey from religion as law to spirituality as wisdom, from morality to mysticism. It is the journey into the Sacred Feminine.

Truthfully, this vision is not new at all; it is the way of seeing that which was taught two thousand years ago by Jesus, what he called the kingdom of God. The vision was so radical – *we are one with God and one with our neighbour* – that not many people understood the full implications of what he said. Even his closest followers kept missing the point. Peter asks, *How often do we have to forgive, is it seven times?* Jesus answers *Not seven, but seventy times seven.* He is forced to keep asking his disciples, *Are you still without perception?* The same is true of us, but one person who did seem to grasp exactly what he was saying was Mary.

Mary Immaculate

I'm always amazed when I see families look at new born babies and can identify a physical likeness, to Mum, Dad, or someone else. Beyond physical resemblance we know how often children grow up to reflect the values of their parents. We have no knowledge of the physical appearance of Jesus but I think the Gospels give us an interesting comment on how Jesus, like all of us, grew and matured as a human being:

> When they had finished everything required by the law of the Lord, they returned to Galilee, to their own town of Nazareth. The child grew and became strong, filled with wisdom; and the favour of God was upon him.[73]

Luke's Gospel has already informed us in his account of the Annunciation that Mary, too, was full of grace and favour with God. The Gospel relates the story of Jesus at the age of twelve, listening to the teachers of the law who express amazement at his wisdom and knowledge. Surely his growth in wisdom will have come from both God and his parents, especially his mother. Isn't this what we mean by the Dogma of the Immaculate Conception? He had to have an extraordinary mother who didn't pass on to him any of the pain and garbage that everyone else experiences in this imperfect world. We all carry the woundedness of our parents and their parents

73 Lk 2:39

before them and that is why we fail to believe that we are loved unconditionally by God. We struggle with the idea of worthiness.

Too often, original sin is misunderstood as a personal guilt. In fact, it is a collective wound that all of us inherit as members of the human race. It goes to the root of our identity which is one of the fundamentals of the spiritual journey. Original sin describes the forgetfulness of our lives. We forget who we are in God and live a separate existence. Original sin is not the result of breaking a moral code; it is living an unconscious life, forgetting who we are. Mary lived a fully conscious life, a life lived in the fullness of grace, a totally aware life. She was fully conscious that she was loved unconditionally by God and surrendered herself to the truth of that mystery. Confronted by the incredible message of the angel she was able to say, *Let it be.* She couldn't possibly work out what was happening to her in her mind. She accepted it in her loving heart, totally open to the mysterious ways of God. She would have passed on this loving wisdom perfectly to Jesus. She becomes the mother of wisdom because she does not try to work it out in her head but accepts the mystery growing in her body. In comparison, our own parents can only do this imperfectly; they inevitably pass on their own fears to us, which is why we all have this deep sense of unworthiness before God and we struggle with suffering. In the case of Mary she was able to teach Jesus not to be afraid of pain and suffering.

We all carry what Eckhart Tolle calls a *pain body* that holds all the accumulated hurts of our lives, including those from our imperfect parents and teachers and others we meet in life. It is this *pain body* which comes to the fore in the transition from first-half of life to the second-half, which explains why there is no set chronological time for this transition, even though for most of us it happens in the middle years of our lives. We have already noted the spiritual maturity of young people such as Dominic Savio and Laura Vicuna. Many young handicapped children are already in the second-half of life; the same is true of some youthful refugees I have met.

Learning how to deal with our *pain body* is at the heart of spirituality. Mary was told from the very beginning of Jesus' life that a sword would pierce her heart because of her child. Even in the manger Jesus is given the gift of myrrh, a perfume to anoint the dead. Jesus, Mary and Joseph become refugees, exiled from their own land. Without great love, great suffering, or prayer, we cannot really deal with pain. It is pain that opens our hearts so that compassion can flow in. Unless we learn how to let the pain teach us, we will become embittered and seek to push the pain on to others. As Richard Rohr says, *What we don't transform we transmit.* Mary's total openness to God's love allows her to stand at the foot of the Cross and say nothing, to hold the pain within and transform it into compassion and forgiveness just as Jesus does. There the Immaculate mother becomes the mother of compassion, embracing everyone.

Mary, Active and Contemplative

When we read the Gospels we notice that after every message that she receives Mary doesn't voice an opinion. There is no quick judgement or reaction; instead she ponders things in her heart. This is a contemplative spirituality. She takes everything into her heart. Heart-knowing is a contemplative way of looking at reality. It doesn't exclude the head – at the Annunciation Mary asks the angel some very practical questions – but it unites both head and heart. We talk about women's intuition which is not so much analytical knowing as an embodied, cellular way of knowing. It is body-based and held there with patience.

Contemplative prayer provides a place of healing for the *pain body.* Instead of being caught up in our thoughts and emotions we learn to detach and become the inner witness, the inner observer, the watcher. As soon as we can do that, we have created a space which lessens the power of the emotions. There is nothing wrong with having emotions; the problem arises when the emotions have me. That is possession, and explains why Jesus spent so much of his ministry healing people who were possessed in all sorts of ways with their addictions and emotions. The most common form of addiction today is not drugs, or alcohol but the addiction to our own way of thinking, our own point of view. Regular practice of contemplative prayer helps to lessen this addiction and opens us to the spaciousness of non-judgmental compassion. We tend to think that other people are the problem; in fact, we are our own problem. If we really want to change others for the better with our various apostolic activities, we have to learn to change ourselves first.

If the Annunciation marks out Mary as a contemplative, the Visitation demonstrates how her contemplation flows into action. This pattern of action and contemplation is perfectly illustrated in Mary's Magnificat which has the same structure as the Beatitudes given by Jesus. Before Jesus speaks about working for peace and justice he addresses the crucial inner attitudes that should always inform such work. He praises poverty and humility. I don't think he is saying that poverty is good; he is talking about an inner attitude of stripping ourselves of our egotistical point of view. In her Magnificat, Mary does exactly the same, uniting the inner and the outer journey.

Salesian spirituality is sometimes criticised as being a bit *childish.* We try to create a fun-loving environment for our young people and some might ask, how deep is that? Anyone who has worked as an educator of the young will know that no education can take place without discipline and hard work. But the fun aspect is a key part of this because it points to the gift of joy that comes from knowing that we are loved unconditionally by God. In recent years Western education has gone down the path of ever increasing tests, targets, and league tables of success or failure. We all want the best academic education for our young people but Don Bosco knew that the best education would take place in an atmosphere of warmth, respect and love. Our mantra has been that we educate by evangelising and we evangelise by educating. This is where our relational spirituality comes to the fore. Young people need to be challenged by adults, as well as encouraged. It is interesting to see that as well as inviting us into a relationship of love of God, Jesus also on a number of occasions commands us to love. It is like encouraging children to eat well. Junk food doesn't really help healthy growth in our bodies; in the same way, if we don't learn through the school of love, our souls won't grow into wisdom.

That is why the Preventive System requires that we do the first-half of life well by providing our young people with a safe, happy and healthy environment in which to grow in mind, body and soul. We need to challenge our young people, to make demands of them and this is the necessary masculine dimension of the Preventive System. At the same time, all this takes place in a climate of love not fear, so that the young will be given a taste of the loving-kindness of God. Compassionate loving is the necessary feminine side of our spirituality. If the young have genuinely experienced loving-kindness and compassion, they will be able to better deal with the wounds and contradictions that all of us experience in life.

As the Mother of Sorrows, Mary is the model for this part of the journey but at the same time she is the Mother of Joy. To experience true joy and peace we have to go through the pain and come out of the other side with the pain transformed, which is what Mary teaches us. Fun experiences may not have a lot of depth about them; but in the second-half of life they are transformed into that joy and peace that is pure gift, a gift that the world cannot really understand because it comes not from external entertainment and stimulus, but from within. It is a contemplative gift.

> I have said these things to you so that my joy may be in you, and that your joy may be complete.[74]

We know the suffering in Mary's life, but we also need to see her as a woman of great joy. I'm sure she brought great joy to Elizabeth as she prepared for the birth of her baby. At the wedding feast of Cana, it was Mary who expressed concern that the wine had run out, and I'm sure she joined in the dancing rather than sitting like a wallflower.

Mary, Help of Christians

The difficulty with this much-loved title of ours is the problem of exclusion or the problem of selection. It seems to suggest that Mary helps only Christians, in the same way that the phrase *chosen people* suggests that God did not love the Egyptians, or other races. There are also many examples

74 Jn 15:11

in the scripture of God choosing certain people: Abraham, Moses, David, Jeremiah, Jonah, Sara, Ruth and so on. There is the choosing of Israel as a people, the choosing of the twelve apostles, and we can include the choosing of Mary.

It appears that God needs images, he needs people who are not just doing their own thing, but God's thing. It doesn't mean that he loves others any the less. In fact, many of the ones chosen in the bible are often quite flawed and wounded people, so that it becomes evident that their power and holiness is not their own. It appears that God wants to choose some people to show that he chooses everybody; they are visual aids of what he is doing in the whole of humanity. The point of exclusivity seems to be inclusivity. Peter finally learns this truth when he is in the second-half of life in one of the most important and explosive statements in the scriptures:

> Peter fairly exploded with his good news: *It's God's own truth, nothing could be plainer: God plays no favourites! It makes no difference who you are or where you are from – if you want God and are ready to do as he says, the door is open. The Message he sent to the children of Israel – that through Jesus Christ everything is being put together again – well, he's doing it everywhere, among everyone.*[75]

A spirituality for today has to be inclusive as we work with all people and all faiths.

The Sacred Feminine

In these liminal times in which we are living, a new force is rising within humanity: the Divine Feminine or the Sacred Feminine, and it is beginning to transform our lives. It is rooted in interconnectedness, in harmony and in equality. I think that if we can live our Salesian Preventive System fully, we can achieve a healthy balance between the active and contemplative life. We can then become conduits for this new consciousness that is emerging as we connect our individual stories, our community stories and our planetary stories.

Many Catholic schools promote a pro-life culture in terms of protecting unborn life. The Sacred Feminine is challenging us

---

75 Acts 10 34-36 *The Message* translated by Eugene E Peterson (Navpress Colorado 2003)

to embrace honour and respect all life so that we can begin to question the violence at the heart of our culture. Pro-life means that we love life all the way from the womb to the tomb. Back in the late 1970s, Cardinal Bernadin of Chicago warned of the need for consistency in the defence of life. In the past our Christian countries have been all too quick to resort to war, to right what we perceive as *wrongs*. Our weaponry today is so destructive that we need to find new ways of promoting peaceful solutions to our problems and disagreements. Needless to say a contemplative practice that takes us into our inner room where everything is one, will help promote a new climate of peace-building. The emergence of the Sacred Feminine in our times is asking for models of cooperation rather than competition.

We are learning to take seriously the rights of excluded groups: women, homosexuals, refugees, those of different faiths, not forgetting the needs of our environment and planet. This is not a feminist agenda because the emergence of the Sacred Feminine needs to achieve union with the Sacred Masculine. What I think will emerge is a new respect and cooperation between science and mysticism, between action and contemplation, between technological and spiritual power. Instead of dominating and exploiting the planet we will learn to reverence creation and see the divine presence in every aspect of created life. This is not New Age religion; it is as old as the scriptures and we see it reflected in Paul's letter to the Colossians:

> We look at this Son and we see God's original purpose in everything created. For everything, absolutely everything, above and below, visible and invisible, rank after rank, after rank of angels – everything got started in him and finds its purpose in him. He was there before any of it came into existence and holds it all together right up to this moment. And when it comes to the Church, he organises and holds it together like a head does a body.
>
> He was supreme in the beginning and – leading the resurrection parade – he is supreme in the end. From beginning to end he is there, towering far above everything, everyone. So spacious is he, so roomy, that everything of God finds its proper place

> in him without crowding. Not only that but all the broken and dislocated pieces of the universe – people and things, animals and atoms – get properly fixed and fit together in vibrant harmonies, all because of his death, his blood that poured down from the Cross.[76]

We know that the Holy Mystery that we call God includes and transcends all gender. The special role of Mary is to be for us the most familiar and comforting image of God's unconditional love: maternal love. When she asked the angel how she could give birth to a son to be called Jesus she was told that the Holy Spirit would overshadow her and make the impossible possible. We are also called to *give birth* to the divine image within ourselves as the mystics remind us. The gift is already given. All we have to do is get our egos out of the way and let God grow within us. That is the wisdom that surrounds us and our fragmented age seems to be aching for. As Salesians, we are called to offer this emerging dream to our young people who will hopefully keep it alive.

In order to live in the second-half of life we have to keep recognising our shadow side. This is a long way from fluffy spirituality. It calls for a radical humility that grounds us in the truth that whatever we judge and condemn in others can be found in ourselves. We cannot get to the joy of the Resurrection without the pain of the Cross. The Sacred Feminine is the gracious heart-space where this pain can be transformed into forgiveness. Mary Immaculate can teach us how to surrender to the generous mercy of God without fear, and as Help of all people she can teach us how to include everyone in non-dual compassion and loving-kindness.

76 Col 1.15-20

Appendix

Centering Prayer

1. Sit still and straight with slow, natural breathing, eyes closed or lowered.
2. Be lovingly present to the God within.
3. If you are distracted by a thought or emotion simply let it go.
4. Use your sacred word to return gently to God.

Twenty minutes is all it takes, but you have to remain faithful to the practice each day. If you can't find twenty minutes try fifteen, or even ten. If you forget, return to it the next day.

If you develop a regular habit you may want to try two periods of twenty minutes a day.

Never evaluate your prayer.

You don't initiate prayer; you join the continuous prayer of the Trinity.

Be still and know that I am God

Other Books by Michael Cunningham

LET YOUR HEART PRAY

LOST AND FOUND Spirituality in a changing world

A TIME FOR COMPASSION A Spirituality for Today

WITHIN & WITHOUT Renewing Religious Life

TREASURE WITHIN

Other Don Bosco Publications

A LENTEN SWATCH A prayer book for young people

SWATCH & PRAY New concept prayer book for the young

SCHOOL ETHOS & CHAPLAINCY

THE CHRISTIAN TEACHER

CHRISTIAN LEADERSHIP

ORDINARY WAYS

TRUST THE ROAD

VIA LUCIS The Stations of the Resurrection

STARTING AGAIN FROM DON BOSCO

SERVING THE YOUNG Our Catholic Schools Today

SEAN DEVEREUX - A life given for Africa

DON BOSCO'S GOSPEL WAY Reflections on Don Bosco

SYMBOLS and SPIRITUALITY reflecting on John's Gospel

LENTEN SUNDAYS

MOVING ON Book of reflective poetry

MAMMA MARGARET The Life of Don Bosco's Mother

DON'T ORGANISE MY TEARS Reflections on bereavement

PRAYERS TO START MY DAY

PRAYERS TO CLOSE MY DAY

To order go to

www.don-bosco-publications.co.uk

or email **joyce@salesians.org.uk**